EARTH BOUND

EARTH BOUND

Daily Meditations for All Seasons

BRIAN NELSON

SKINNER HOUSE BOOKS

BOSTON

Cover design by Kimberly Glyder.

Text design by Suzanne Morgan.

Printed in the United States.

print ISBN: 978-1-55896-465-5
eBook ISBN: 978-1-55896-664-2

10 9 8 7 6 5 4 3 2
14 13 12 11

Library of Congress Cataloging-in-Publication Data

Nelson, Brian, 1958-
  Earth bound : daily meditations for all seasons / Brian Nelson.
      p. cm.
  ISBN 1-55896-465-7 (alk. paper)
    1. Meditations. 2.Nature—Religious aspects—Meditations.
I. Title.

BL624.2.N45 2004
204'.32—dc22

                                        2003067349

PREFACE

In Michelle Huneven's novel *Jamesland*, a Unitarian Universalist minister named Helen is out snorkeling with some friends when a whale appears. It's not a touchy-feely moment. While the encounter with the leviathan does leave some of her friends rapturous, Helen herself reels from the beast in something like terror and spends the rest of the day grappling with her experience: "Curled against the wall on her bunk, Helen understood why God did not make full-frontal appearances to humans. A single whale was too much to bear."

Many of us have ecstatic exchanges with nature. Others, like Huneven's heroine, connect with creation warily at best. Still others we might call nature-based agnostics—hearing tales of the power of the earth, unable to deny it might be possible, but seeing no evidence of it in their own experience.

Earth Bound addresses all these groups with 366 reflections on nature in all its guises: the animal and plant kingdoms, the senses and capacities of the human body, the biosphere of Earth, inner space and outer space, and humanity's poetry and prose about its relationship to creation. This book aspires to speak equally with environmentalists, pagans, religious liberals, and general readers. For those who revere nature already,

Earth Bound offers a celebration. For those more cautious about the cosmos, *Earth Bound* offers a meditation.

Let this book point out aspects of nature that you have overlooked or forgotten. The energy that resides within everything offers itself up to you for inspiration and renewal. *Earth Bound* can help focus that attention.

Of course the universe regards the concept of "a year" with suspicion. We constantly fuss with our calendars to align them with the cycles of existence. Given that, you don't have to start using this book on January 1. You can begin on any day. You can read a month at a time, sampling the text when you feel the need, or use this book as a resource for your daily spiritual practice. You can even read it all in one fell swoop, treating yourself to an intensive seminar of the senses.

This planet is our home, our heritage, our future—a truth that can never be spoken enough. Whenever you dive into the ocean, wander in the woods, or lie on your back and stare at the stars, you are forging a connection to truth. And if Frank Lloyd Wright was correct when he argued, "Nature is the only body of God that we shall ever see," then both this book and life itself are filled with prayers.

January

JANUARY 1

On this day people commonly make resolutions to change their behavior. Self-improvement is a worthy goal, of course—but in nature, the eagle and the swan don't appraise themselves and resolve to be perfect from this point forward.

"Perfection" is actually a human concept that the rest of nature may well ignore. From the human perspective, "perfection" is often thought of in terms of symmetry, but nothing in the world is truly symmetrical. More and more people are abandoning the classical ideal of perfect symmetry and, instead, focusing on appreciating Nature as it is. Think, for example, about the difference between modern dance and ballet—while ballet urges dancers to go beyond their physicality toward abstract perfection, modern dance celebrates the body as it is. So go ahead, resolve to be a perfect person—but acknowledge that your flaws are what make you part of nature.

As Leonard Cohen sings, "There is a crack in everything . . . that's where the light comes in."

JANUARY 2

Pagan communities celebrated Yuletide for twelve days, a festival that comes to an end today. This tradition may have begun in Egypt, when the celebration of the god Horus lasted twelve days. Like so many other pagan traditions, it was later folded into Christianity as the Twelve Days of Christmas, which end on Twelfth Night (January 6), also called Epiphany.

Many pagan traditions employed natural elements to symbolize their close connection with the natural world. Celtic Druids of the second century B.C. used mistletoe as a burnt offering to mark the start of winter, hanging sprigs in homes as a token of good luck or a sign to welcome travelers. The Scandinavians also revered mistletoe, believing it sacred to Frigga, the Norse goddess of love. That belief is still with us in our holiday tradition of kissing under mistletoe. Kiss someone under the mistletoe, and consider that you are part of a chain of affection stretching back millennia.

JANUARY 3

The famous naturalist John Muir tells of riding an avalanche in Yosemite. While he doesn't recommend the practice as particularly safe, he never forgot the experience of being borne along helplessly by a force of nature:

"This flight in what might be called a milky way of snow-stars," he wrote, "was the most spiritual and exhilarating of all the modes of motion I have ever experienced. Elijah's flight in a chariot of fire could hardly have been more gloriously exciting."

Granted, you may not want to repeat Muir's experience. But on a lesser scale, Earth stands ready to give us glimpses of heaven. All it takes is seizing such moments as they are offered.

JANUARY 4

Today our planet is at *perihelion*, that point in Earth's orbit at which it is closest to the sun. It's not an event you're likely to notice, but it's one of the subtle geometries that enfold us every day and make life possible on earth.

When you look up at the stars tonight, think about what their orbits might mean for you. Take note of their patterns and symmetry. Appreciate the beauty and complexity of the universe.

JANUARY 5

The Aztec goddess Tonantzin was associated with both winter and the moon, a striking combination. Few phenomena transform the earth for us like the sight of snow under the moon, suffusing the landscape with so much light that you can read a book at midnight. A full moon and a snow-covered field seem as though they are in witty conversation—reflecting brilliance back at each other.

What do they talk about, the moon and the snow? Perhaps they're in competition, each trying to outshine the other. More likely, they glory in the results of their collaboration. Together, the moon and the snow reveal new dimensions of hillsides we have taken for granted, fields we have forgotten. Perhaps, in this transformation, a goddess truly is at work.

JANUARY 6

Today Italy celebrates *La Befana*, the kind witch who brings toys to children. Some legends say Befana comes late in the holiday season because she has been too busy cleaning her house to come earlier. This folklore, sexist though it is, still works the pagan crone into holiday celebrations. Without wise women minding their hearths in the old country ways, there might well be no holiday to celebrate.

Today is also celebrated across much of the world as the Feast of the Epiphany, the day the wise men departed from the infant Christ to spread his message of light and life. Although we often call them kings, they were *magi*, astronomer priests, finding their calling in the stars.

A holy outsider and students of the wild, Befana and the Magi remind us that we are made holy ourselves as we clean our hearths and look to the heavens.

JANUARY 7

When we think of flowers, our thoughts turn to spring, but winter has its own bouquet to offer. Though they may not be as flashy as the blossoms of spring, plants and flowering herbs like foxglove and ground-cherry are still to be found in winter fields. From woodlands to beaches and salt marshes, many plants and flowers thrive in this season of cold.

There are always the familiar poinsettia and holly to brighten hearths at this time of year. But nature is persistent and brings us new riches even when we least expect them.

JANUARY 8

Today marks the birthday of famed cosmologist Stephen Hawking. In such works as *A Brief History of Time* and *The Universe in a Nutshell*, Hawking has expanded not only our understanding of creation but of human potential as well.

Speaking on his sixtieth birthday, Hawking told an audience at Cambridge University that nothing compares to the moment of "Eureka!"—the instant when a new revelation makes another piece of the universe comprehensible.

The joy of discovery is truly unparalleled. Keep searching.

JANUARY 9

Caroline Herschel, the first woman to discover a comet, died on this day in 1848. With her brother John, she discovered the planet Uranus. Her fellow astronomer, Maria Mitchell, said of her, "Every line she wrote was an argument for the higher education of women."

Mitchell herself was a noted astronomer who was happiest atop her home, scanning the skies for new discoveries. Nearly two hundred years ago, space was viewed as an exclusively male domain, but Herschel and Mitchell helped us to see that the cosmos doesn't play favorites.

The heavens await us! Whether the astronomers are the Herschels, Mitchells, Hubbles, or our own daughters and sons, each day we can find more stars to wish upon.

JANUARY 10

On this day in 1969, the photograph *Earthrise* was published in *Life* magazine. The picture was taken by William Anders, an astronaut on the Apollo 8 mission, who writes about that moment in *A View from Space*: "We'd come 240,000 miles to see the moon, and it was the Earth that was really worth looking at."

As people around the world saw the planet from a distance for the first time, a fundamental shift in human consciousness began. Certainly we knew that Earth was not the center of the universe from a scientific perspective, but to actually *see* our globe hanging there in space had a startling effect on *Life's* readers. Quickly the term *Spaceship Earth* became popular, as we recognized both the beauty and the fragility of our true place in the cosmos.

Every time you see a photograph of the earth, remind yourself that we are *all* in the picture.

JANUARY 11

Amelia Earhart became the first woman to fly solo across the Pacific Ocean on this date in 1935. In flight for more than eighteen hours, Earhart was more alone than most people ever are. Suspended high above trackless waves, often hundreds and even thousands of miles from civilization, she endured a loneliness that few can imagine.

Yet in isolation the smallest things become paramount. About opening a Thermos in the middle of her journey, Earhart remarks, "Indeed, that was the most interesting cup of hot chocolate I have ever had, sitting up eight thousand feet over the middle of the Pacific Ocean, quite alone." As we enjoy our own cups of cocoa in these winter days, we might consider what it would take for us to appreciate them quite as much as Earhart did.

JANUARY 12

"No snowflake in an avalanche ever feels responsible," writes Stanislaw Jerzy Lec.

Eleven thousand inhabitants of the Pacific island of Tuvalu will be forced to leave their tiny island over the next fifty years as it is swallowed by the rising sea, one of the first large-scale casualties of global warming.

No one feels responsible for Tuvalu, but we know there are cars we drive, products we use, and companies we patronize that are damaging our world. Yet it's not too late to do something. We don't have to be snowflakes borne along by the pull of events. We can create our own avalanches. Marge Piercy's poem, "The Low Road," traces events from the will of a single person to the power of a committee, a community, a convention, a country. "It goes on one at a time," she explains, "it starts when you care to act."

JANUARY 13

The white herons invisible in the snow. The beer can crushed by the roadside.

The crunch of your shoes in the snow, magnified by the winter stillness. The devastation wrought by an ice storm, throwing cars and lives off the road.

The crackle of icicles as a squirrel runs along a tree branch.

Is it all equally precious? Can we embrace both the beautiful and the terrible? What do we gain from it? Robert Penn Warren writes, "We must try to love so well the world that we may believe, in the end, in God."

JANUARY 14

Today we honor the birth of Dr. Albert Schweitzer, the Unitarian theologian and humanitarian who argued for reverence toward all life. Opposing the brutal philosophy of Nietzsche, Schweitzer affirmed that love for our fellow beings really can redeem the world.

"When we have a choice," he writes, "we must avoid bringing torment and injury into the life of another, even the lowliest creature; to do so is to renounce our manhood and shoulder a guilt which nothing justifies."

And of course we do have a choice—far more often than we realize. Make your choice today.

JANUARY 15

Dr. Martin Luther King, Jr., the historic leader in the American civil rights and anti-war movements, was born on this date in 1929. As he accepted the Nobel Peace Prize in 1964, King marveled at the resources we have available to us and at how far we have to go to give all people their fair share.

King asked his audience, "Why should there be hunger and privation in any land, in any city, at any table when man has the resources and the scientific know-how to provide all mankind with the basic necessities of life?" Surveying both the grandeur of the earth and the accomplishments of science, King observed, "There is no deficit in human resources; the deficit is in human will."

Today's preachers and prophets won't let us forget King's message. Today, tomorrow, or next week, you might find it in yourself to spread the word.

JANUARY 16

Harp seals are born with entirely white fur. Their fur turns spotted grey when they are old enough to care for themselves. This extraordinary evolutionary tactic helps the baby harp seal blend into the arctic environment and evade capture when it is most vulnerable.

We too should change as we grow older—and feel no shame about it. Our culture values staunchness and consistency. We berate politicians for changing their views. But shouldn't we want them to accommodate their opinions to what they learn in life? Should we ask our friends to stay the same forever? As Emerson writes, "A foolish consistency is the hobgoblin of little minds."

Change when you have to. If the harp seal can do it, so can you.

JANUARY 17

On this date in 1994, Northridge, California, was struck by the most damaging earthquake in the United States since the 1906 San Francisco quake. In some homes, the noise and rumbling were so intense that people believed it was the end of the world. Families stumbled out of their homes, avoiding broken glass in the darkness, and met their neighbors out on the street. They instantly formed teams to shut off gas valves and check on the missing.

While the Northridge quake was a sobering reminder of the power of the earth, it was also an important example of the strength of ordinary people. Many didn't really know their neighbors well, but they didn't hesitate to help each other even though they were terrified.

During the Cold War Rod Serling wrote dark dramas about citizens turning on each other when apocalypse loomed. But we have survived as a species because of our natural ability to work together under stress. Say hello to a neighbor today, and celebrate the neighborhood that is our planet.

JANUARY 18

Captain James Cook stumbled upon a bit of paradise on this date in 1778. He named these tropical islands after the first lord of the British Admiralty, the Earl of Sandwich. But they were not known as the Sandwich Islands for long because they had been settled long before Cook sailed the Pacific. Soon enough they were known by the name their inhabitants called them, *Hawaii.*

When we believe we have discovered something new we can never be sure someone else hasn't uncovered it already. But as we name our discoveries, it's wise, at least, to recall that names are not to be confused with the wonder of the things they describe. Today, as an experiment, walk outside and try to forget the names of all the things you behold. Take pleasure instead in seeing them as they truly are.

JANUARY 19

Vesuvius, Etna, and Krakatoa—these are the volcanos that loom large in the popular imagination. But the greatest volcanic eruption in recorded history took place on this date in Iceland.

In 1783, four cubic miles of lava spewed from a cone in the Icelandic wilderness.

Imagine the red-hot lava against the frozen backdrop. During the winter months, many people clamp down their souls just as they have fastened the shutters against blizzards. They become icy and still in order to conserve their energy during this demanding time of year. If you're one of those souls, don't risk an eruption. Instead, take an extra nap, enjoy a hot cider—create for yourself an early thaw.

JANUARY 20

In Robert Frost's famous poem "Stopping By Woods on a Snowy Evening," he tells of watching the drifts grow in a quiet and lonely wood. "The woods are lovely, dark and deep," he writes, "but I have promises to keep."

Despite the miles the poet has "yet to go," he's made time to sit still and take in the snowfall on the darkest night of the year. Indeed, there's something appealing and even seductive about that darkness. Some may forget their promises and linger forever in the woods. Others may avoid the woods entirely, for fear they'll be swayed from their commitments.

No matter how many miles we have to go before we sleep, it matters that we take a moment to drink in the darkness and calm that surrounds us.

JANUARY 21

Gary Paulsen's memoir *Winterdance* describes a man running the Iditarod, the Alaskan dog team race, only to vanish. Everyone thought he'd fallen through a patch of sea ice and drowned, and Paulsen drilled himself in remembering details about the man to share with his bereaved friends and relations.

But the man survived. The ice on which he had been racing broke off from the mainland, a crag so huge that the man didn't notice that he was lost for an entire day. He was rescued at last, but got no credit (or brass belt buckle) for finishing the race. But Paulsen says, "He didn't care. He'd found god out there on the ice alone."

Is the divine waiting outside for you, too? Religious seekers throughout history have undertaken pilgrimages in search of revelation. If you're having trouble reaching your destination, consider that sometimes the best way to find it is to get lost.

JANUARY 22

Fanny Bullock Workman—an adventurer and explorer in a time when women were not expected to be either—died on this date in 1937. She bicycled across Spain and trekked into the Indian Himalayas in wide skirts and hobnailed boots.

In her explorations and writings Bullock Workman demonstrated that the unknown need not daunt us. We can venture out into *terra incognita* with spirit and wisdom and come back with stories that dazzle the imagination. In fact, the more obstacles we face, the more we may learn, and the more we will savor it. Onward!

JANUARY 23

For all its beauty, a street coated with ice forms a palpable threat if we try to navigate it. But ice also preserves.

The intense cold slows down our heartbeats, sometimes saving lives. It also saves a record of the past. Scientists working in Antarctica have found evidence of global warming by drilling down into the ice and studying the cores they remove.

Ice lets us journey back in time. The past is not dead—not completely. Traces of an earlier world lie all over the planet, frozen in ice.

JANUARY 24

In Robert Hayden's lyrical poem, "Those Winter Sundays," the poet's father trudges out into the "blue-black cold" to raise a fire before anyone else gets up. It is hard and thankless work that adds to the cracks and aches in the father's skin. "What did I know," the poet asks, "of love's austere and lonely offices?"

In late January, when the smallest kindness is a valiant triumph against the weather, take heed of what austere and lonely offices others do for you—and think well on what you can do to return the favors.

JANUARY 25

"How full of the creative genius is the air in which these are generated! I should hardly admire them more if real stars fell and lodged on my coat." Thus wrote Henry David Thoreau on the special characteristics of snowflakes, thousands upon thousands of distinct crystalline structures that descend upon us every winter.

When was the last time you walked outside and let a snowflake land on your palm, so that you could hold it up to the light and see its unique structure?

Nature is a sculptor, but too often we're running through the sculpture gallery on our way to the gift shop. Maybe winter has a special genius in making it cold outside—the better to slow us down and make us appreciate the distinct difference in each day.

JANUARY 26

You may not be able to turn in a paper, get to class on time, or attend a meeting because of a January blizzard. The vast blankets of snow will seem a rude obstacle to your life, one more example of nature's inconvenient disregard for your schedule. You may curse the weather for its lack of consideration.

But years from now you won't remember the contents of that paper, the subject of that class, nor the matter of that meeting. You may remember the drama as the city was coated with a blanket of glorious white, the silent beauty that brought the frenzy of the day to a standstill.

Don't let your attachment to the details of your day keep you from taking in the glory of nature at work around you. The earth doesn't care about your appointments and deadlines. Let that be a gift.

JANUARY 27

David Attenborough begins *The Life of Mammals* by describing an Arctic waste that appears barren of all life. Yet even here, he reveals, the ice is honeycombed with storerooms and bedrooms, the living quarters of tiny lemmings. With ingenuity and persistence they scan their surroundings for a seed or a blade of grass, treasures that enable them to hang on until the thaw.

No matter how destitute and devoid of life the winter barrens may seem—no matter how isolated and lonely the desert, the plains, or even the suburb—there is always hidden life teeming, using its brains and its heart to keep hope alive. You can find it in your own backyard.

JANUARY 28

This date marks the birthday of Auguste Piccard (1884), who tested the limits for travel. Piccard set records in ballooning even as he gathered data about the intensity of cosmic rays in the stratosphere. Then he built his own bathyscaph, descending thousands of meters into the sea.

This date also marks the death of the first Challenger shuttle astronauts. At their funeral, President Ronald Reagan read the poem "High Flight" by John G. Magee, Jr. The poet "slips the surly bonds of Earth," and spirals through space to "put out my hand and touch the face of God." Whether we are among the stars, deep in ocean depths, or lost in uncharted wilderness, perhaps the eyes of God can always see us.

JANUARY 29

As this month draws to a close, remember that the name of January itself comes to us from the two-faced Roman god Janus. Janus holds a special place as the god who is able to look behind him and before him at the same time, learning from the past even as he plans for the future.

Janus is also the god of doorways, bridges, and harbors. As such he stands between, in the margin, in the boundary. Our culture constantly asks us to be in or out, to be on one side or the other. January and Janus teach us there is something to be learned in the gray areas.

JANUARY 30

When we think of Maryland we think of crab fishermen and the Chesapeake Bay. When we talk of Texas we talk of sagebrush and oil fields. But there are also mountains in Maryland, and there are piney woods in Texas.

No location on earth can be reduced to a single characteristic. Every place holds more secrets, more treasures, more marvels than have yet been discovered—even the field behind a parking lot is a wilderness waiting to be explored.

Whenever you think you know a place, look more deeply.

How do tiny animals survive the long persistent cold of winter? Bernd Heinrich studied them closely and described what he saw in *Winter World: The Ingenuity of Animal Survival.* He observed caterpillars manufacturing a kind of antifreeze to survive the winter, bees staying in perpetual motion to keep their hives just above freezing, golden-crowned kinglets defying the unwritten rule that only large animals should live in the freezing north.

It all requires persistence and ingenuity, unlikely-seeming qualities in the slow-moving creatures of this season. But that same persistence and ingenuity, that ability to create one's own warmth and sustenance, can inspire us to weather this season and emerge stronger than before. Birds do it, bees do it—so can we.

February

FEBRUARY 1

Today marks the beginning of the Celtic pagan festival of Imbolc, which derives from the Gaelic word *oimelc*, meaning "ewe's milk." Nature-based theologies associate this time of year with the moments just before dawn.

Like the Celts, the ancient Greeks also described the cycle of the seasons with myth. In Greek lore, Persephone, the daughter of harvest goddess Demeter, was kidnapped by and married to the underworld god Hades. While Demeter mourned the absence of her daughter the earth endured winter, echoing Demeter's grief. But finally a deal was struck, allowing Persephone to spend half the year above the surface of the earth with her mother (spring and summer), and half (autumn and winter) in the subterranean empire of her new husband.

Today we celebrate the promise that Persephone will return. Look outside—a promise is waiting for you.

FEBRUARY 2

The newest part of the Imbolc tradition is Groundhog Day. German folklore held that a modest creature of the earth, emerging from its winter burrow, might be frightened off by the sight of his shadow amid the half-light. The critter's reaction was a bellwether: If it ran, there would be six more weeks of winter. If it stayed, an early spring was imminent.

The six-week figure was not accidental, since Imbolc is balanced roughly six weeks between the winter solstice and the spring equinox. But for most of us it doesn't matter whether there will be six more weeks of winter or not. We can put on another sweater or throw more logs on the fire if need be. The true wisdom of Groundhog Day is in its exhortation to study the small things—the comings and goings of nature's humblest creatures. What we learn from them may tell us what's in store for us all.

FEBRUARY 3

One of the ancient traditions of this time of year is to call out to the Goddess—Persephone, Gaia, or any other deity who embodies the fullness of the earth. By honoring the Goddess people invite her to return and bring spring.

We can celebrate the Goddess today in various ways. A poem might suffice, offered up by a lone soul within a sacred circle in the middle of the woods. Perhaps a dance would do the trick—performed to a ballad that has particular meaning to the celebrant, or improvised in harmony with the music of the spheres. A gathering of friends might summon the Goddess—especially if the right cider is served.

Invoking the holy is one of humankind's oldest traditions, and it needn't wait for a Sunday or a special moment. The earth is always listening.

FEBRUARY 4

We're so used to seeing (and creating with kindergarten origami) the typical six-pointed symmetrical snowflake. But snow crystals can form in many different shapes—hollow columns, needles, asymmetrical leaf-like forms, and still more. This accounts for the many different qualities of snow—some packs are fluffy, while others are dense and hard.

In 1954, Ukichiro Nakaya published a study of snowflakes that brought their immense variety into public awareness. In addition to the lovely examples, Nakaya told us about the curious and odd cases. "Snow crystals," he writes, "are the hieroglyphs sent from the sky." Decoding the hieroglyphs teaches us that creation embraces all kinds of beauty—both the conventional and the unusual.

FEBRUARY 5

"Other seasons come abruptly but ask so little when they do," writes Verlyn Klinkenborg in *The Rural Life*. "Winter is the only one that has to be relearned."

Winter is no picnic to be sure. Spring doesn't insist that we scrape all the walkways to keep ourselves from falling and breaking a hip. Summer doesn't require us to pull the batteries out of our cars so that they don't freeze overnight. Autumn doesn't freeze our beards.

Yet when all is said and done, winter knows what it's doing. It won't be ignored. It requires us to be present. This is the season's gift to us.

FEBRUARY 6

Maybe it's the winter blues. Or maybe it's seasonal affective disorder. But for many, the winter is a difficult time, a time of depression and lethargy. Listen closely to your heart and your body in this time, and make use of the comforts of the season if you're ailing.

Firesides, the company of friends, song and drink—these make great graphics for holiday cards. But if we're succumbing to winter blues, they could also be the stuff of survival. The American ethos urges people to be daring and to persevere no matter what. But nature trumps our plans. Your senses and your body are subject to its whims. Keep alive to the messages of the sun, the wind, and your own heart during this season.

FEBRUARY 7

In this season when the nights are longer, perhaps we should be thinking of ourselves as explorers.

"Turned away from the sun," writes Diane Ackerman in *A Natural History of the Senses*, "we see the dawning of far-flung galaxies." The glare of the day star keeps us geocentric, focused on our own world, but when the night takes hold, our gaze is aimed away from the gravitational center of our own solar system, out toward the frontiers. Night is an obstacle for many activities—but it's also an opportunity.

Now that the winter requires us to spend more time in darkness and restricts our activities with inclement weather, discover the joys that have eluded you in the blinding brilliance of summer.

FEBRUARY 8

Beneath the ground, the seeds are slumbering. During these months, seeds are like time bombs, filled with explosive energy that they will only release at the proper moment.

You yourself may be one of these seeds. Perhaps you need a period of rest before you can capitalize on all the power inside you. Or perhaps that dormancy is already ending, and it's time for you to burst forth. Like any seed, make sure that you get all the light and the nutrients you need. Prepare the ground around you, and take steps to distract any creatures that would feed upon you before you've reached your full potential. Then start blossoming.

FEBRUARY 9

Jane Yolen's beautiful children's book *Owl Moon* tells the story of a girl and her father who go out looking for owls. It describes how the care and quiet that are needed to spot an owl in the middle of the forest bring father and daughter closer.

We often think about venturing into nature alone— perhaps inspired by dramatic tales of adventurers pitting themselves against the wilderness. Today ask someone to come with you. Whether our fellow travelers are our children, our parents, our lovers, our friends, or even strangers, whom would we not love better, having explored the wild alongside them?

FEBRUARY 10

Penguins didn't dress up in "tuxedos" to become mascots for formal wear companies. Their remarkable coloring serves a very different purpose—their black feathers help them to find each other on land while their white undersides help them to blend in with the ice. Looking like part of the glacial mass helps them evade the seagoing predators who look at them only from below.

Look closely at your own "tuxedos"—not simply what you wear, but how you present yourself to the world. Do you comport yourself in such a way as to help your friends find you in empty times? Do you know when to blend in for safety, and when to ruffle your feathers in play? You may have natural qualities—a great laugh, a sharp eye, a strong arm—that help you flourish. But while penguins, alone in the wild, cannot afford to ignore their natural traits, we sometimes blind ourselves to our own resources. Reappraise yourself, and make the most of your own unique capacities.

FEBRUARY 11

Belladonna was used by Italian women in centuries past to dilate their pupils, thus making them more attractive and giving the herb its name, "beautiful woman." But belladonna is also a poison, and women who used it may have numbed their senses as well.

Dilated eyes are considered a sign of beauty as well as innocence—yet someone who is poisoning herself to achieve that appearance can hardly be called innocent. And if we use nature's secrets only to turn the focus back on ourselves, aren't we cheating both ourselves and nature? What would it take to recapture the innocence with which you once looked at the world? What would it take to open your vision again to the world as it is?

FEBRUARY 12

Today is one of several festival days throughout the year that are devoted to Diana, the Roman goddess of the forests and the hunt. Ancient myths told of pilgrims who, wandering in the woods, came across the naked goddess. Angry because she was embarrassed, Diana changed the hapless strangers into forest creatures, stripping from them the trappings of civilization. Yet many people today work hard to shed the nice patina of manners with which society has burdened them. We often yearn for an idealized, "simpler" life, but how far should we pursue it?

Would Diana's transformation be a punishment or a gift for you? The wild calls to all of us, and we each must decide how to answer it.

FEBRUARY 13

The Japanese have a party idea perfect for these cold winter nights. In the tradition called *kumikoh*, various samples of different incense are prepared, and guests are asked to sample the scents and compete to identify them. In an advanced version of the game, guests also write down a literary or cultural reference pertaining to the scent, or write a poem in praise of it.

The tradition is first recorded in *The Tale of Genji*, the thousand-year-old poetic epic of court romance by Lady Murasaki Shikabu. It's a chance to tune up your senses, sit by the fire, and maybe engage in a little courtly romance of your own. It's the earth that provides all these sensations—weave them into the poetry of your days.

FEBRUARY 14

On Valentine's Day we hear a lot about Venus, the Roman goddess of love and beauty. Botticelli paints her arising from the sea, born like a pearl from a shell, tresses flowing lightly through the air like clouds.

Consider the notion that that love and beauty spring from the ocean. When we go swimming, perhaps we are communing with the font of human affection. When we work to preserve the oceans, perhaps we are acting as devotees of primal beauty. And when we recognize that our bodies are composed largely of salt water, perhaps we acknowledge our spiritual bond with the source of all life.

What spirits of love course through you? What beauty lies within you, unrecognized?

FEBRUARY 15

Legend has it that ancient Rome, one of the greatest civilizations in history, was founded by two brothers who were raised and suckled by a wolf after they were abandoned in the wilderness. To the world, Rome represented the pinnacle of human achievement, but a primal connection to nature was at the heart of its mythology.

In ancient times today was the rite of Lupercal, whose name honors that mother wolf. It was a rite of purification and fertility that was later adopted by the Catholic Church and re-christened as the Feast of the Purification of the Virgin Mary. The pristine simplicity of our connection to nature is a kind of purity. The wilderness can nurture us even as it did the infant founders of Rome—and in its care, we are all newborns.

FEBRUARY 16

On the website of the Poker Flat Research Range in Fairbanks, Alaska, a visitor poses a curious question. "I seem to recall seeing aurora a long time ago . . . did I?"

So few people actually see the aurora, the remarkable displays of the light that occur as solar wind brushes up against our planet's magnetic field. We're more likely to have seen them in a film shown in a middle school science class than to have experienced the real thing. But on certain occasions over the years, aurorae have been visible far outside the normal geographic range, so it's possible that you might have seen one if you were in the right place at the right time.

But it's also touching that the question is worded so tentatively. Our childhood memories of nature are so delicate, yet they're also hardy enough that they often refuse to desert us completely. What will it take for you to rekindle them?

FEBRUARY 17

On this day in 1917, a street in Baltimore was the first anywhere to be lit with gas. This was the beginning of a curse for astronomers, who would come to revile city lights for interfering with their telescopes. Yet it had its advantages, as well. It made the night a safer place and helped bring people together from their isolated hearths to a new appreciation of the evening.

Do the lights that we turn on at night separate us from nature or let us enjoy it in a new aspect? The answer will be different for everyone. Tonight, take a step outside and ask yourself how much light you really need. Soon the days will be longer, so savor the night now—by taking your light into your own hands.

FEBRUARY 18

When their valentines didn't work out as planned people often turned to the earth for assistance. The old

English folk song, "Scarborough Fair," supplied one recipe; the herbs parsley, sage, rosemary and thyme were all folk cures to aid love, lust, marriage, fertility, and fidelity. Legend has it that placing vervain in your mouth and kissing your beloved while reciting a Latin spell will make you irresistible.

But perhaps the specific herbs are immaterial. Perhaps the secret of such remedies is that they pull us into the immediate rich life of the wild. Is anything more attractive than that? What passions can you unlock as you grow closer to the earth?

FEBRUARY 19

Today is the birthday of Nicolas Copernicus. The Polish astronomer dared to assert that the earth revolved around the sun, when the entire spirit of his time affirmed that the Earth was the center of the universe.

What do you believe simply because you've been told—and what have you taken the care to investigate firsthand? What would you do if all your observations of the world contradicted what others had taught you all your life? Can nature itself give you the courage to believe what it tells you?

FEBRUARY 20

Nature photographer Ansel Adams was born on this date, and it's no exaggeration to say that the American environment owes him a debt. For thousands upon thousands of people who have never been to Monument Valley, Adams' majestic portraits of our wilderness give them a window into a new world and help conservationists recruit new support.

Adams typically sets his lens at a distance from his subject in order to take in the entire expanse—a technique that yielded panoramic vistas but threatened to isolate the viewer from the view.

Don't settle for hanging a picture on your wall. Enter the landscape yourself whenever you can. You are part of the picture.

FEBRUARY 21

In wintertime, huddled up in our homes, scents can be among our best friends. They're keys to memory, due to the connection between olfactory organs and the primitive, limbic system of the brain. After too many months of inclement weather the insides of our homes can start to feel oppressive. Aromas can transport us safely away.

Make some room for the scents of pines and other evergreens, oranges and other citrus fruits, and rich spices like cinnamon. By bringing nature into your home, you can remind yourself that the outdoors will be ready to welcome you back when the sun comes out again.

FEBRUARY 22

In the old fairy tales princes were always being turned into frogs, and princesses who wanted husbands were always being asked to kiss them. Maybe this is a Jungian parable about love—how it requires that you accept the animal within people if you want to enjoy their more civilized attributes as well.

Perhaps we should consider every frog a prince. Start to think in different terms—deem every dog a duke and every cat a countess, regard every rabbit as royalty and every mosquito a monarch. What if we stopped judging the earth as a place of untidy wildness in need of human dominion—and instead bowed to nature's nobility?

FEBRUARY 23

In prehistoric times some species of dragonflies grew to have wingspans well over two feet in diameter. Imagine such a thing: a whizzing, buzzing king of insects, making his way through the world without any of the boundary issues that keep latter-day birds from getting too close to us. Such goliaths would deeply unsettle our house pets, provide a boon for pest control experts, and revise our whole notion of the food chain.

Today, dragonflies are still striking—without striking fear. They skim through the air as mere shadows of their ancestors. When you see a dragonfly, it bears a message: All is not as it once was; the mighty can be brought low. Yet at the same time, the simple fact of the dragonfly's survival, even in a diminutive form, teaches another lesson as well—that the resourceful and adaptive can survive no matter what.

FEBRUARY 24

The massive redwood trees of California are so large that ten people, with their arms outstretched, touching finger-to-finger, cannot encompass them. They are the largest living things on the planet, and older than the Bible. The biggest of the sequoias, named the "General Sherman Tree," is as wide as a blue whale and far taller than any other creature on earth; estimates place the tree's age between three and four thousand years.

The redwoods offer an inspiring symbol not only to conservation movements but to millions of tourists every year. The deeper our roots, the higher we may grow.

FEBRUARY 25

The central character in Leo Lionni's children's book, *A Color of Its Own*, is a very confused chameleon. He despairs because he seems so inconstant—he's green when he's on the leaves, purple when he's in the heather. It's only when he meets another chameleon that he realizes his skin doesn't define him—what matters is his connection with a friend.

Sometimes we all go too far in blending into our environments, and we lose track of the traits that make us unique. If the demands of your life are taking a toll on you, don't work harder at blending in. Reach out instead.

FEBRUARY 26

If you have ever been ice skating, you know that a residue of ice is left on each blade afterward, like loose jewels on the metal. It's there because one doesn't really skate on the ice. The blades carve a small path into the frozen surface, and so it's more accurate to say that one is skating in the ice.

We often think that we must skate *over* our troubles, as if they weren't there. But perhaps we'll be happier if we can learn to skate *in* our dilemmas. We can dance as we deal with it all.

FEBRUARY 27

It's late winter, nesting season for peregrine falcons in the skyscrapers of New York City.

Long on the endangered species list, these marvelous birds of prey are slowly making a comeback in the concrete canyons of Manhattan, of all places. The wide array of smaller birds in the city gives them plenty of food, and the towering skyscrapers and suspension bridges give them unique perches and plenty of space to dive and hunt. Add the natural tendency of New Yorkers to live-and-let-live, which allows the birds to build their homes unmolested by curiosity seekers, and Manhattan suddenly seems the most natural nesting place of all for these birds.

Look around your own city or suburb; there may be wonders of nature that you never expected. But as you come across them, remember to live—and to let them live.

FEBRUARY 28

Though it may not seem like it, the sun is returning, the days are growing longer, and this pagan season of Imbolc invites us to celebrate. The fire goddesses are rejoicing.

Light a fire yourself. It takes some doing to lay a good fire, one that doesn't just fizzle out after a few bright flames. Practice building fires; it's a skill that will warm your home with more than just heat.

As you watch the blaze grow, consider that the fire goddesses are always virgins, symbolizing limitless potential. The future is beckoning, and with the proper fiery spirit, you can achieve whatever you plan.

FEBRUARY 29

Nature defies our calendars. We're constantly adding nanoseconds to our atomic clocks to keep them in tune with the spinning heavens. And every four years, the Western world has to catch up by a whole day—Leap Day.

Leap Day makes us aware of the silliness of our pre-occupation with time. People born on Leap Day find themselves in the ridiculous situation of having a birth-day only every four years. Consider poor Frederick in *The Pirates of Penzance*, a Leap Year baby who's inden-tured to pirates until his twenty-first birthday—which means he won't be free until he's eighty-four! Clearly the only time we really need to keep track of is *now*.

March

MARCH 1

Yellowstone National Park was established on this date in 1872. President Ulysses S. Grant set aside this remarkable enclave of natural wonders "for the enjoyment of the people." In a century known for its rapacious exploitation of the environment, this declaration stands apart, a historic date in our relationship with the earth.

Yellowstone and other natural treasures call out to us in their uniqueness, in their fragility as well as in their strength. As Alice Walker writes, "Anything we love can be saved." Consider today what wonders of the world, large or small, summon love from you—and what can be done to preserve them. The more we care for the delicate marvels of the planet, the more we care for ourselves.

MARCH 2

"There's joy in the mountains, there's life in the fountains," says William Wordsworth in his poem "Written in March." As spring approaches we all look forward to new energy, warm breezes, and renewed pleasure in the outdoors. But be careful. It's easy for the habits of winter to keep you shuttered up in your study, in spite of all your good intentions.

Muscles become locked when they're clenched too long, and sometimes the reflex of staying inside during the winter is hard to relax. There's been something nurturing and cozy in hibernation, in cuddling by the fire and enjoying the hearth. Yet now the earth is shaking off its snowy mantle, and so should we all. Just as Wordsworth's fountains can only flow freely when they're no longer paralyzed by ice, now we have our chance to warm up to the larger world again.

MARCH 3

March is known for "coming in like a lion and going out like a lamb." The winds of the month are proverbially fierce right now, dying down to gentle breezes by the time April is nearly here. So quick, while the siroccos are still strong, take a moment to step outside and embrace the wind.

Winds bring us smells from other places, set the trees in motion, invigorate us, and propel us. Inspiration, of course, has as its etymology the idea of "spirit," or wind. The more that wind breathes through you—whether it be the Holy Spirit, the breath of the divine, or just a good strong March gale—the more your soul may be opened.

MARCH 4

If it hasn't begun already, the beginning of the Christian season of Lent will soon be commemorated on Ash Wednesday. On this day Catholics mark their foreheads with the ashes of the burnt palm leaves left over from last year's Palm Sunday services, but even non-Christians can identify with something primal and earth-based in daubing one's forehead with ashes.

The practice of wearing ashes predates Jesus and is described in the Old Testament on several occasions. It was part of a ritual of mortification and fasting, humbly purifying oneself for the year ahead. As we move toward the heightened activity of spring, such a practice may make us appreciate the world's budding energy all the more acutely.

Consider what you might burn, what you can do without. To what might you say goodbye as you prepare for the activity of the new season?

MARCH 5

What if the Garden of Eden was underwater?

What if the snake tempted us to leave the nurturing embrace of the oceans, to pick the apples that were growing on the shore? What if the whole Eden story is a metaphorical account of our evolution from the seas? Certainly at the dawn of time, we did leave the ocean, even though we weighed less there, even though childbirth was easier there, even though everything in the seas flowed to us so naturally.

With spring approaching, maybe it's time to revisit the Garden. Take a long warm bath and reconnect with that wonderful, warm floating feeling that was our species' first habitat. Pour in milk, orange juice, and mint, seed your bath with rose petals, orange peels, and smooth stones. Scent it with sandalwood, violet, and rosemary. Light candles; play music. Sit. Soak. Simmer. A small paradise is still within reach.

MARCH 6

The smell of spring is arriving. The animals can sense it, and maybe you can feel it. Smells weigh only nanograms, and yet we are so finely attuned to the natural world that these slight somethings still register on both our senses and our souls.

Look to the air around you. Consider how it holds portents of the months to come: the aromas of budding flowers and the musky gusts from the nests and dens of awakening animals. Consider, too, how it contains the markers of days gone by: last fall's fruit that fell to the ground before harvesting, a bit of must left over from the rains, the traces of perfume from a visitor last week. The very air holds clues to the future and the past.

MARCH 7

Bioethicist Willard Gaylin writes, "An individual human being is only a useful social myth." Take away the nurturing that any of us receives from our family, from our society, from our planet, and you'll have a person who isn't quite as human. We rely for our very humanity on touch from other people—on laughter—on sunlight—on things that we cannot generate within ourselves.

As you emerge from your hibernations to begin spring planting or start your spring cleaning, take this time to restore your connections to the larger world. Run your hands along the bark of a tree, walk your pets, leave out some birdseed, embrace a friend, and shake the hand of a stranger.

MARCH 8

The great Brazilian composer Antonio Carlos Jobim's "The Waters of March" is a wonderful piece of music for this month. A catalog of the small phenomena that greet us each day, it includes both the sweet and the unsettling, the unique and the ugly. Jobim allegedly wrote it while building a wall on his property, a task made more difficult by the rainstorms that undermined his efforts whenever he thought he'd made progress. He found himself frustrated, yet undeniably charmed, by the river waters that teased him as he worked.

The song's last stanza reads in English, "And the riverbank talks of the waters of March, it's the end of all strain, it's the joy in your heart."

Where is your river? What is it saying?

MARCH 9

Before we ever sent astronauts into space, human beings wanted to prove that it would be possible to survive at such altitudes and to land without catastrophe. As Scott Ryan describes in his book, *The Pre-Astronauts*, centuries ago a few daredevils went exploring in a direction previously out of range: up.

They flew above the stratosphere in manned balloons, using air tanks to survive where the air was simply too thin. And then, to prove that humans could sustain re-entries, one man jumped from the balloon—in a parachute from the edge of space itself, falling so fast that he broke the sound barrier!

When you feel that you are falling you may actually be exploring. Not every plunge is a problem.

MARCH 10

You can hear them morning, noon, and night, calling to each other, getting the work of this new year underway. The birds are returning, scavenging your neighborhood to make their homes, building cradles for their young, ceaselessly flying onward to the next task.

Terry Tempest Williams writes, "I pray to the birds because they remind me of what I love rather than what I fear." Robins, blue jays, and wrens are the priests of springtime, confidently going about their rituals, selflessly offering inspiration, never resting upon their laurels (or elms or maples). Enter their green cathedral and sing a song of praise to the new season along with them.

MARCH 11

Today is recognized as Johnny Appleseed Day, in honor of a man who lived within nature as he felt called to do.

So many myths and legends have sprung up around John Chapman that it is impossible to know where the facts begin, but we do know that acres and acres of apple orchards throughout the Ohio Valley owe their existence to Chapman's efforts.

There are Johnny Appleseeds among us today. While they have not yet achieved legendary status, that's not their goal (nor was it Chapman's). They are the women and men who live simply on the land, bartering for resources, trying to spread nature's plenty. Look around the next time you adventure into the wild; you may see them. You may even be one of them. What seeds for the future can you sow today?

MARCH 12

Around this time of year the full moon is the Worm Moon. There's a great poetry to the naming of many moons—Hunter Moon, Wolf Moon, Snow Moon. But . . . Worm Moon?

Yet if we adjust our gaze downward, into the earth from which all things spring, we can find value and poetry even in the lowly worm. The worm tills the soil, threading its way through the dirt, loosening it and enriching it for the planting of crops. The worm is a valuable ally as the year wends around to spring and the sowing of seeds.

With the next full moon, take a moment and give thanks for all the small, unseen forces that conspire, for reasons of their own, to make our lives more livable.

MARCH 13

The equinox is nearing. Ever since late December the earth has been inclining toward a new balance. Rebecca Parker urges us, "Let this be the time we wake to life, as spring wakes, in the moment of winter solstice." Whether you began recovering your balance at that moment of solstice, or whether you are only awakening now to the possibilities of spring, it is never too late to begin again.

Look to the thawing waters and break the frozen sea within you. Look to the ripening buds on the trees and let tender life grow inside you. Look to your own spirit, yearning for newness, and encourage it to come out and play.

MARCH 14

We all ask it when we're children: "Why is the sky blue?"

For centuries, nobody knew—until a man, born on this date in 1879, refused to stop asking the questions he wondered about as a child. Albert Einstein grew up to explain, in a 1910 paper on the phenomenon he called "critical opalescence," how light is scattered through the sky by individual molecules.

Remember the questions about creation that you asked as a child—and don't give up on finding the answers.

MARCH 15

"Beware the ides of March," Caesar was warned. The ides is the midpoint of the month in the old Roman calendar. March, May, July, and October all had their ides on the fifteenth. Other months were shorter, with their ides on the thirteenth.

In Zeno's paradox, we are always at the midpoint—the arrow travels halfway closer to its target every time it moves, and therefore, arguably, it never reaches its destination. It's possible we're always at the midpoint, never really reaching what we think are our goals, and that every seeming arrival is simply another midpoint in a journey to someplace else. Take one more look at where you're going, and enjoy the trip.

MARCH 16

"I'd rather be a forest than a street," writes Paul Simon in his song "El Condor Pasa." But perhaps the biggest choice offered in the lyrics is not between two types of existence—sparrow or snail, hammer or nail. Perhaps the biggest question is raised by the next lyric: "Yes I would . . . if I could."

Are you so sure you *can't* decide to be a forest rather than a street? If Whitman can tell us, "I am large . . . I contain multitudes," then maybe it's up to you whether you're a forest or a street. Maybe it's a false dichotomy, and you can be a forest when you feel like it, a street when it suits you. You have both forest and street within you—travel them whenever the urge strikes you.

MARCH 17

Images of leprechauns, magical creatures who live in the earth and play tricks on humans, are a staple of Saint Patrick's Day. Yet like many legends, the leprechauns may have their basis in fact. In the so-called Dark Ages, it is believed that Lapps sailed across the sea from Lapland to make their homes on the warmer Emerald Isle. As they did in their native land, the Lapps—who were markedly shorter than the Irish—hollowed out homes under the sod.

The ways of the Lapps were mysterious to the natives and may have given rise to the legends of leprechauns. The ways of others often seem incomprehensible to us. Today, learn more about a tradition that seems alien to you. Perhaps you'll find magic in it.

MARCH 18

At about this time every year, the swallows return to San Juan Capistrano, a small California town famed throughout the country for this connection to nature.

San Juan Capistrano's special place in our culture is assured, but we can all do something in our own neighborhoods to live more harmoniously with nature. We might start by watching and listening more closely—there are probably connections between our homes and the earth that we have not appreciated before. The more we celebrate the small wonders that manifest themselves in our own corners of the planet, the more at home we feel.

MARCH 19

This week Iranians celebrate Noruz, the Persian New Year. The focus of the festival is on nature itself, symbolized by a ceremonial plate laden with foods and spices that all begin with the Persian letter *Sin* (S). Sprouts or lentils represent rebirth, a wheat pudding symbolizes patience, and an apple represents health and beauty. The lotus fruit symbolizes love, garlic represents health, sumac evokes the color of sunrise, and vinegar reminds us of age and wisdom.

Other traditional items in the ritual include coins for prosperity, eggs for fertility, flowers for freshness, and a goldfish for life itself. It all adds up to an elegant statement that creation began on the first day of spring. Whether or not we celebrate in this fashion ourselves, we shouldn't miss out on this perfect day to honor creation.

MARCH 20

The Vernal Equinox generally begins tonight, when the day and the night fall into perfect balance. It's the beginning of the growing season, a time of rebirth and fertility in which the Saxons celebrate their nature deity, Eostre.

Easter takes its name from Eostre, goddess of rebirth, and so it is no accident that Jesus' own rebirth takes place in this season as well. Easter retains deep ties to the natural cycle—we never know its date from year to year, because it falls on the first Sunday following the first full moon after the Vernal Equinox.

Look, therefore, for opportunities to throw away the calendar and make plans instead in harmony with the cycles you see in the universe. Today, at least, honor the equinox and seek out balance.

MARCH 21

Around this time each March, visitors to Washington, D.C., anticipate the National Cherry Blossom Festival, hoping to glory in the natural spectacle of these delicate, evanescent blooms. But if they don't plan it just right, the tourists will miss out, for cherry trees bloom quickly and only briefly before the blossoms scatter to the winds and the full beauty of this time has vanished for another year.

The turning point of spring is like that; if you blink you may miss it. It takes a vigilant and patient eye at times, to enjoy nature in all its splendor. The moments we prize are often fleeting, and perhaps they are best so.

MARCH 22

Spring cleaning: For some, it's a chore born of routine, while for others, it's a chance to start fresh and to gather energy.

Many of us clean almost every day, but most days the task is merely about maintenance. Only at this time of year is there a special resonance to the job—an anticipation of the future, a cleaning away of last year's detritus. Spring cleaning is also a kind of soul-cleaning, a chance to invest not just in dustrags and shelf paper, but in the future. Our home is not only the place where we collapse at the end of the day, of course, but also a receptacle for our energies and dreams. Spring cleaning may give those dreams a little bit of fresh air even as it connects us to the immediate.

MARCH 23

As vines sprout, as flowers bud, and as plants make their way across your lawn, take a moment to learn from their ability to adapt to any number of conditions, to germinate and grow even when all the odds seem stacked against them.

Some plants can sow their seeds only when there's fire or smoke in the vicinity; they've learned to survive when other greens have been charred to nothingness. Some trees have evolved to endure remarkable extremes of both heat and cold.

We can be as adaptable as the plants if we can treat obstacles as the conditions for growth. The spring invites us to try.

MARCH 24

In the American colonies some three hundred years ago, this would have been New Year's Eve. Julian calendars in use at the time marked the days and months differently—George Washington considered his birthday to be February 11, and it was only changed to the 22nd when we adopted the Gregorian calendar in the eighteenth century.

If you considered tomorrow to be a New Year, are there habits you'd want to consider over and done tonight? Do you have projects that can begin afresh tomorrow? Every day, of course, is both an ending and a beginning. So prepare for a new adventure tomorrow, free from the burdens you can release today.

MARCH 25

Spring fever is an old expression that many of us may not take seriously. But when it comes to lions and tigers and bears—oh, my! Many animal species are genetically programmed to mate in the spring so that their offspring will be born at a time when there's plenty of food. Other creatures, especially sea creatures, mate at the full moon, when the strength of the tide guarantees safety for their young.

If our own genetic heritage frees us from any pressure toward seasonal romance, why does pop music constantly warble about spring fever and the magic of the moon? Perhaps because deep down we know that we are losing something powerful when we ignore the seasons. Perhaps studying the next full moon this March will make you fall in love again—with the power of the earth.

MARCH 26

The rivers are flowing strongly now, liberated from winter's ice. The wild freedom of a river, of a spring breeze, of a bird in flight, is the same freedom we ourselves celebrate when we leave behind our habits and walk or swim with no plan other than the sheer doing of it.

"Do you think," writes Yemeni poet Nadja Awad, "that the elements do what they are supposed to do and not what they want to do?" Of course not. Find a moment when you yourself can forget about what you're supposed to do, and revel instead in the wild. Your plans will keep. Throw them aside for today, and follow the rivers, follow the winds, follow your dancing heart.

MARCH 27

The poet Dante Alighieri sets the opening of his *Divine Comedy* on Good Friday in the middle of a metaphorical dark forest: "Midway through this life's journey, I found myself in a dark wood where the path had disappeared. It is difficult to speak about that thick and savage wood; the thought of it brings back fear so bitter, death scarcely seems worse!"

A true woodsman will notice that Dante's description of this forest is remarkably vague. And he's not vague because he's writing an allegory; even if the wood is only figurative, a man who writes one hundred cantos cannot be accused of lacking in imaginative detail. Perhaps if Dante had taken the time to observe the woods about him with more care, he would not have ended up having to trudge through Hell and Purgatory to end up safely again. We end up lost when we look at the whole forest; it is only by studying the individual trees that we will find our way home again.

MARCH 28

"Is there such a thing as God?" David Rankin asks in his poem "Natural Theology." As evidence, he offers a sunrise and a blooming lily.

Are the sunrise and the lily the proof of God? Or are they each part of God themselves?

Or is God in the watching, in our ability to appreciate these beautiful phenomena in the first place?

Keep your eyes open to the sunrises and your own answers may dawn.

MARCH 29

Imagine the difficulty you might have believing in giraffes if you had never heard of or seen one. There was some doubt about the whole proposition in the imperial Chinese court of the early thirteenth century, until the admiral Cheng Ho brought a live giraffe back to China from Africa. Thereafter giraffes were considered avatars of luck.

These days it's hard to imagine ourselves in the place of those Chinese courtiers. We all know what giraffes look like, even if they are not native to our part of the world. But the variety of life on this planet is infinite. Today, take a moment to appreciate the creativity of nature.

MARCH 30

Consider the spring buds on the leaves, the new flowers that have bloomed—so many of them in places you considered played out, exhausted. We can never underestimate the earth's capacity to nurture life even where it appears to be tapped out.

And consider, too, the ways in which corners of your own heart are alive, no matter how many heartbreaks they have endured. We have all witnessed tragedies, we have all mourned, yet we find the will to continue. Give your spirit credit for its ability to renew itself even after terrible damage.

In the words of Wendell Berry, "Practice resurrection."

MARCH 31

Passover seders are on their way, if not already taking place. The foods used in these meals evoke the suffering and faith of the Jews in ancient times.

Would it be easier just to talk about the Jewish heritage, rather than to gather this odd and diverse assortment of foods? Why experience the bitterness of slavery with the taste of horseradish, for example?

Yet by using the primal materials of nature, we learn deep lessons—lessons not only about the past but about the immediate. As Rabbi Mordechai Kamenetzky writes, "At the Seder, we train ourselves to find meaning in the simple things of life."

April

APRIL 1

April itself may fool us more than once. The brilliant traces of spring appear one day, and next day they're dashed into puddles.

Sara Teasdale wondered at April's beauty, so poignant that she hated the idea of leaving the glories of spring behind when she died. In her poem "Blue Squills," she asked the trees and flowers to burn her, to hurt her— "wound me, that I through endless sleep may bear the scar of you." It's a startling request. We think of nature as only helping us with its gifts and inspirations. But nature is also a sculptor who wears away at us day by day—and perhaps we are blessed by the traces that creation leaves upon us, evidence of a life well and fully lived.

APRIL 2

Sacred cows are far more sacred than most people realize. According to the Hindu religion, 330 million gods and goddesses, the vast pantheon of deities that oversee the heavens and the earth, are housed within the body of the humble cow.

Our own culture, which sees cows largely as disposable food sources, could not be more opposed to such a view. We might ask ourselves how two such impressive cultures have reached such divergent opinions about so unpretentious a creature, about how have we grown so different, and what can bring us back together. As American religions start to take ecological stewardship seriously, they might seek common ground in the *dharma*, the act of moral honor, that the Hindus undertake in caring for the modest cow.

APRIL 3

Unitarian poet e. e. cummings writes of "Just-spring, when the world is mud-luscious" and "puddle-wonderful." In his "Chanson Innocent, I," boys run around playing marbles, girls jump rope, and the "goat-footed balloonMan whistles" somewhere, the song of Just-spring wending its way through everyone's heart.

The mention of the goat-footed vendor evokes the Greek god Pan, the music of the wilderness. There is a kind of "panic" in Just-spring, in these early days when all the pent-up energy of the winter suddenly bursts forth and runs riot. Take note of it. Don't discourage it. It is the birthright of April.

APRIL 4

If it's true that April showers bring May flowers, then why are so many people glum about spring rains? For some it's a touch of seasonal affective disorder, the deprivation of sunshine that casts people into the blues, while others are discouraged by the disruption in their schedules and/or the inconvenience of tramping through the mud.

But the grass, leaves, and flowers obviously welcome the downpours. Thirsty after a hard winter, they drink long and well. Are you spiritually parched? Each April shower is an invitation to all nature to drink deeply, to savor the abundance of the world. Make sure you give yourself the same opportunity to nourish your roots.

APRIL 5

Children often ask, "Why do roses have thorns?" A common answer is that it discourages animals from eating them. But any child who lives near the woods knows that rosebushes aren't well protected by thorns; deer come along and eat the roses whenever they get a chance. Children will see that the whole thorn strategy isn't working and may even suggest that roses should start growing thorns right on their petals.

It's tempting to demand a reason why it should be painful to handle a beautiful flower. But engaging fully with nature requires a degree of risk.

APRIL 6

Today marks the day that Robert Peary, Matthew Henson, and their team reached the North Pole—or what we call the North Pole now.

Geologists have observed that lava flows inside the earth may be working to realign the planet's magnetic field. If it happens, the South Pole would become the North Pole. Compasses would point in the opposite direction! While this magnetic reversal is believed to have happened several times in the life of our planet, it hasn't yet happened within recorded history.

Such a reversal would be a great setback for anyone who wants to believe in certain geological constants. The next time you refer to the North Star as true, remember that the only real constant is change—and celebrate it.

APRIL 7

As bumblebees go buzzing through your garden this spring, take a close look at them—well, maybe not *too* close—but just close enough to see if they really do have knees.

In the 1920s, "the bee's knees" was a common description of excellence and wonder. The true marvel of the bumblebee isn't in its leg joints, of course. We can admire its tirelessness, or its passion, or its ingenuity in hooking its wings together to make a single surface. Most interestingly, there's an urban legend stating that bumblebees shouldn't be able to fly because of their aerodynamic design.

How easy is it to believe a clever story rather than the evidence of one's eyes? Maybe, just maybe, we humans ought to start questioning the conventional wisdom that we can't fly either.

APRIL 8

Because the almond tree flowers before it bears fruit, some cultures have regarded it as a symbol of hope, but others see its blossom pattern as a warning against haste.

As new projects develop this spring, some will hail them automatically for the hope they promise. Others will reflexively regard any new idea as too much, too soon. Perhaps we need universities to offer courses in Spring Studies, in the nurturing of new life. It takes vision and discretion to tell the difference between the numinous and the mere novelty.

APRIL 9

Many people know that whales sing—but do you know they have a repertoire?

David Attenborough, in his remarkable survey *Life on Earth*, testifies that when whales return to Hawaii each spring, they sing different songs than they did the previous spring. Old themes have vanished from their melodies, to be replaced with new material.

Are you still cycling through the same old themes? Now that it's spring, will you haul out the old familiar chestnuts or compose new tunes?

APRIL 10

On this date in 1872, the first Arbor Day summoned the citizens of Nebraska, which desperately needed windbreaks, to plant over a million trees in a single day. Imagine the power of this accomplishment. When those midwesterners went to bed that night, they knew that the ache in their limbs came from giving a gift to the earth, and woke up the next day knowing that the very color of the landscape had changed for the better, thanks to the work of their hands.

The poetry of Arbor Day lies not just in the beauty of a tree—but in the connection between ourselves and the forests we nurture.

APRIL 11

There are seventy-six species of opossum in this country—and nearly as many folktales about them. They do *not* hang from their tails all day. They do *not* curl up around their mothers in orderly fashion. And they most certainly do *not* procreate by rubbing their noses together. Yet all of these are myths that have been bandied about for generations.

When something—or someone—looks as strange as an opossum, maybe we can't help but spin tales about it to explain how odd it is. Everything that is foreign walks among us laden with the weight of our apprehensions and groundless speculations. We must take the time and care to see living things and people for what they really are.

APRIL 12

As the days get longer and the temperatures get warmer, animals start shedding the fur that helps them weather the winter and hoard their body heat. Unless they shed this fur, they'll overheat in the months to come.

Similarly, the longer we act as though we're in a winter culture, a culture of scarcity and deprivation, the more likely we are to overheat now that it's spring.

Stop living in a winter of your mind and shed the barriers that keep things at bay. Act as though abundance and generosity are not only possible but imminent. Welcome easier times and they will happen more often.

APRIL 13

In William Wordsworth's famous poem, "I Wandered Lonely as a Cloud," the poet describes a crowd of daffodils: "I gazed—and gazed—but little thought/ What wealth to me the show had brought." The mere memory of the blooms cheers him onward.

The daffodil, a flower as old as recorded history, was ignored for centuries until English gardeners reclaimed it in the seventeenth century. Dismissed as weeds for quite some time, daffodils took back their place of honor in the garden.

We might consider what other treasures are waiting for us in the weeds, offering a memory that can carry us ahead through troubling times.

APRIL 14

Whatever's wrong with this country, it can't be too bad if we have a National Dolphin Day.

On this day, it's a pleasure to celebrate these creatures, with whom, of all the animals on this planet, we share one of the most rewarding bonds.

Eyes also turn to the oceans in other parts of the world on this day, for today also marks the Festival of Maruyama, the Hindu Goddess of the Sea. Between them, these two occasions direct people of both hemispheres to the waters from which we sprang. Find a way today to play in the water as a dolphin does—or simply to appreciate the oceans, lakes, or rivers near you, cradles of all life.

APRIL 15

Last Dinner on the Titanic: Menus and Recipes from the Great Liner, by Rick Archbold and Dana McCauley, reveals that the passengers on the Titanic dined from a menu that reaped the rarest and richest of nature's rewards: Lobster Thermidor, Quail's Eggs in Aspic with Caviar, and Poached Salmon with Dilled Mousseline Sauce and Cucumber.

Did such rich fare help give the survivors the passion for life they needed to endure the catastrophe? Would the food have tasted any better if the passengers had known somehow that it was to be their last meal? The Titanic disaster, which we commemorate today, teaches us both to respect nature's power and to revel in its wonders while we can.

APRIL 16

Walk out on your driveway, or on a sidewalk around your home and study the concrete closely; it's starting to break. The earth will only tolerate tarmac for so long. How do those buds make their way through inches, even feet, of solid industrial paving, to send a few gentle sprouts up to the open air?

Build, raze, or pave how you will, manicure your lawns as you choose, dig swimming pools or raise towers, and yet sooner or later, nature will break through. But this is not a cause for despair at how your plans are being confounded—for you are a part of nature as well. Like these April sprouts, keep growing, keep pushing up through the crevices toward the sun.

APRIL 17

A frequent symbol of vanity is the preening bird. The time it spends in its toilet, grooming, arranging its feathers just so—what a fop! Yet its preening serves two important purposes—not only the attraction of a mate but also a kind of aerodynamic maintenance work. With their wings shaped precisely, birds can execute aerobatic maneuvers that can save their lives. Their preening is not about vanity but survival.

Do you have any vaguely aerobatic maneuvers to execute in your own life? You can fly better if you honor yourself by caring for your body. It doesn't have to be about vanity. It may just increase your chances to survive and to soar.

APRIL 18

This is the beginning of bullfighting season, a tradition that both fascinates and disturbs. The elaborate ritual in which a matador taunts and then dispatches a huge, menacing animal is a feat of bravery to some, craven cruelty to others. Archaeological studies have revealed dancers—both male and female acrobats—capering about with bulls in ancient Crete. The goal was not to kill the animal, but to somersault over its horns, to play with a wild beast, to take risks and emerge unscathed.

How can we reclaim this idea? Ride a horse, dive with a dolphin, dance with a dachshund, caper with a kitten. Meet nature in communion, not in a contest.

APRIL 19

Spring in Unitarian Universalist churches is often the occasion for the flower communion, a unique service which recasts the blood-and-flesh imagery of Christian communion into a ritual that honors nature. Congregants bring flowers to the service, mingle them in the same water, then leave the service with a flower that someone else brought.

Devised by Czech minister Norbert Čapek, the genius of the flower communion is in how it recaptures a rite of spring in which we all engaged as children. Every child picks flowers, trades with each other, and comes out better for the bargain. And one needn't wait for the church calendar to practice this ceremony. You can exchange flowers with friends or family this very day. A wealth of spring bouquets awaits—and their beauty only grows when they are shared.

APRIL 20

Norbert Čapek's brother Karel is best known (especially to crossword solvers) as the author of the robot play *R.U.R.*—but one of his most enduring works couldn't have less to do with robots. In *The Gardener's Year*, Karel Čapek describes the monthly tribulations that face anyone who toils to bring forth beauty from the earth.

"This is one of Nature's mysteries," Čapek explains, "how from the best grass seed most luxuriant and hairy weeds come up; perhaps weed seed ought to be sown and then a nice lawn would result." The devoted gardener pulls up roots and weeds and stones, cherishes the shoots, protects against aphids, and worries about each heavy rain. Čapek shows us that no one is more idealistic than gardeners, for in planting flowers and grass and trees, they also sow hope.

APRIL 21

Bamboo records found in the tomb of an ancient Chinese emperor reveal that a solar eclipse took place on this date in the year 899 B.C. As the ancients wrote, "The sun rose twice today."

An eclipse was a marvel to people of that time. Yet the wonder was greater than they knew. They could never have imagined that, nearly three millennia later, a team of historians, linguists, cosmologists, and computer programmers would work together to verify their observations.

With every orbit of the spheres, with every turn of the heavens, we are connected in awe to generations long gone, and generations yet to come. Look to the skies, and feel the ties that bind us all through time itself.

APRIL 22

The Everglades preservationist Marjorie Stoneman Douglas once remarked that the Earth is as tough as an old shoe. On Earth Day, take comfort in its endurance, its perseverance, and its sheer stubbornness.

We've proved that wetlands can be rehabilitated and endangered species can be saved. Likewise your own spirit, your beleaguered capacity to hope for the future, can be reinvigorated. Walk in the park, climb a mountain, swim in a lake, dig in a garden. Draw strength from the mantle of the planet, a world stronger than all of us put together.

Dream Eden.

APRIL 23

J. M. W. Turner, acclaimed as one of the greatest landscape painters, was born on this date. Turner's magnificent paintings and watercolors do not render the world as it is but rather as he saw it. Scholars debated how far Turner's work diverged from reality; it was clearly not abstract, yet it was too impressionist to be regarded as a faithful representation of the world.

Perhaps Turner's work is more faithful than that of the objectivist painters. In being true to his own vision of nature, perhaps he is more honest. Maybe we compromise our own vision of nature when we speak only of those qualities in nature upon which everyone can agree. Look to the landscape outside your own window, and if you see things that nobody else does, don't doubt them. Treasure them all the more.

APRIL 24

Deep inside the earth, incredible forces are at work. Temperatures of volcanic intensity combine with the weight of vast boulders, bearing down on the rocky mantle of the planet. And from this pressure, gemstones are born. Whether topaz or tourmaline or diamonds, they qualify as gems by meeting standards of beauty, durability, and rarity.

When you sense the heat rising in your own life, consider how it may be turning you into a precious jewel. You will emerge from these troubles more durable and more beautiful for what you have endured—a rare individual.

APRIL 25

The names of some butterflies suggest an almost military pecking order: the Monarch, the Red Admiral, the Silver Skipper. But these beautiful creatures recognize no such hierarchy. They all began as eggs, one no better than the next. Then they hatched into caterpillars, among the lowliest of creatures, inching along patiently in search of food. Each caterpillar then embeds itself in a chrysalis and bides its time until it can emerge winged.

We think that caterpillars transform only once, but from egg to grub to cocoon to butterfly, they've changed three times! Only in the last stage are they considered exemplars of light, beauty, and grace, but they are always engaged in metamorphosis.

If caterpillars are engaged in constant change, how much more so are you, with your varied and complex life? And if caterpillars can become butterflies, think of what you have the potential to become.

APRIL 26

Over a century ago, a strong young man went to live on the Mississippi. He had been born as an illegitimate child in Haiti and came to America mainly to escape conscription into Napoleon's army. He met with failure in America and was even jailed briefly for bankruptcy. Near the end of his rope—with not much more than a rifle and a set of art supplies, he journeyed to the Mississippi River—drawing, painting, and writing about what he saw.

His portraits of birds and other wildlife, coupled with his record of living in the wild, became an instant sensation. His work inspired literally millions to a new reverence for nature, and so on this day we celebrate the birth of John James Audubon, remembering that any of us, faced with adversity, may find the spirit to move ahead, simply by venturing outside our door.

APRIL 27

As the earth blossoms during the month of April, the Aztec goddess Mayahuel, patron of the agave plant, may be looking after us.

For those growing up in the desert the agave is a source of bounty, so much so that Mayahuel is sometimes depicted as having four hundred breasts. The stubborn, hardy agave provides needles and thread. Its fibers can be made into ropes or even poles, and its liquid can provide nourishment, shampoo, a useful poison, and even a good stiff drink.

All around us are riches and resources we are in danger of ignoring because their source is so humble. Look more closely at the plants, the rocks, the planet you have taken for granted. If we open our eyes, Earth provides.

APRIL 28

The Bible tells us that God pledged to Noah that he would never again flood the earth, sealing the covenant with a rainbow.

Now, of course, we understand the rainbow as a natural phenomenon, the spectrum of visible light refracted through raindrops. But there may well be a divine force at work in the universe, communicating through the play of light.

Perhaps rather than walling ourselves up in sanctuaries to pray, we should be spending more time listening to nature. What messages might you hear in a sunbeam and an April shower?

APRIL 29

At this time of year, narcissus flowers are blooming. The name of this beautiful flower comes from the story of Narcissus, a young man who looked into a pool and was so enchanted by his own reflection that he couldn't turn away.

But maybe Narcissus got a bad rap. Even if we can be sure that he was staring at his image rather than some mystery in the depths of the pond, he still deserves a break. After all, a pond isn't the best mirror around. If you gaze into clear water, your features will still be colored, distorted. Maybe Narcissus was distracted not by himself, but by the realization that nature doesn't reflect our own truths back at us in any simple fashion. Possibly we should all consider how we look from nature's viewpoint.

APRIL 30

Kids who watched old Universal horror movies knew all about "Walpurgisnacht." In Gothic tales and creepy short stories, this was the night that all evil in the world ran loose. The Universal studio execs probably never knew that Walpurgis Night is just another name for May Eve or Beltane, the pagan ceremony that celebrates the height of the spring, the fecundity of the earth, and the richness of nature in blossom.

How did this festival of the earth's generosity come to be associated with evil? Nature was a threat to Calvinist thought, which strove to rise above humanity's supposedly base origins. Consider how you may have demonized that within you which is only natural. We are all products of nature—now is the chance to honor, rather than condemn, our bond with the planet.

May

MAY 1

In Lerner and Loewe's *Camelot*, Guinevere sings "It's May, it's May—that darling month when everyone throws self-control away." May Day has ancient roots as a celebration of fertility, of conception and blossoming. The dance of the maypole and the rite of the May Queen are festivities that linger in our ancestral memories.

Does that mean you need to throw self-control away? As Boris Pasternak writes, "Man is born to live, not to prepare for life."

Even if it accomplishes nothing of use, try putting up a maypole, decorating it with ribbons, and letting children dance around it. Celebrate the fullness of spring. Give yourself the chance not just to survive but to thrive.

MAY 2

Preparing a May basket, filled with flowers of all sorts, for an elderly friend or relative, is a long-standing tradition. There is a language of flowers, of course, but the message of a May basket is simple: "I care. I hope that you bloom again."

In some Roman Catholic churches the statue of Mary is garlanded with flowers at this time. In ancient Rome itself the five days surrounding May Day were the

Florifertum, a pageant of flowering beauty in which citizens wore blossoms and wreaths in their hair and flowers hung from every building.

Flowers are not only expressions of nature; they can also express many of our dearest hopes and feelings. Let them speak.

MAY 3

Does your garden reflect you? Is it well-ordered, with every inch accounted for, or is it wild, mangy, untrammeled? Is it neglected, in need of food and light?

Even if you don't garden, look at the way plants around you grow. Perhaps everything is green, but there's a desperate lack of other color. Or perhaps your surroundings are filled with succulents, holding on to their water for a time of need. Maybe you barely see the thriving trees and plants because you're distracted by the empty spaces between them, calling to you for attention.

Gardens can be a kind of Rorschach test, allowing you to see something within yourself. And even if the garden you study is neglected, remember that all gardens are bursting with subtle life, just awaiting more care.

MAY 4

Take a moment today to listen to the birds. If you listen carefully you'll hear their distinctive voices. Scientists have discovered that while birds instinctively want to sing, the particular way they warble is not innate. Baby birds learn their songs from their parents; if you take a bird away from its mother and father, it will learn a wholly different song from some other bird.

Like the birds, we each learn our own songs. We inherit our particular music from others. Is the legacy welcome or unwelcome? Perhaps this is a good day to start writing new songs.

MAY 5

Randall Jarrell's book for children, *The Bat-Poet*, tells of a bat who's not at home among his friends. He's compelled to stay awake during the day and experience the wonders visible in the sunlight. He writes poems about what he's seen—the mockingbird, the owl, the chickadee. But his fellow bats have a hard time understanding these visions of things that are so totally outside of their experience.

It's not always a simple matter to communicate the wonders of nature to someone else, to help someone share your vision. It can also be hard to open your own ears and your heart enough to receive the wisdom that someone is bringing you from a world you have never experienced. Talk to a friend today about how you view the world, and listen also to your friend's own vision.

MAY 6

The medieval world was fascinated by alchemy, enthralled by the idea of turning base metal into gold.

On some level nature itself inspires this obsession. We see with our own eyes that the world is full of startling transformations. The lowly caterpillar becomes a stunning butterly. Bare black trees become glorious celebrations of color. But in a society driven by commerce, alchemists focused on the gold standard, and a transformation that would create wealth. Perhaps they defined wealth too narrowly.

Look to the sky, as it fills with clouds and rain, then clears again; look to the gardens, to the birth cycles of animals. Radical transformations are everywhere, and they require no special alchemical secrets. Change is the only law.

MAY 7

About this time of year, the Ice Hotel in Jukkasjarvi, Sweden, finishes melting into the River Torne. In November each year, the residents of Jukkasjarvi begin rebuilding it. Guest suites, bathrooms, restaurants, even a church, are all carved from the frozen landscape. Somehow the hotel is staffed for nearly half a year and guests are willing to pay to sleep overnight in a structure made from ice.

Ultimately, though, the seasons do their work. Bit by bit, the building melts away. If sublimation is the process of moving directly from ice to water vapor, this is one building that is literally "sublime."

We want our own homes to be more lasting—but can they be equally sublime? The more you draw from nature into your own dwelling, the more it may connect you to the transcendent.

MAY 8

Topophilia means the love of place. For many people today, this may be an abstract concept. In his movie *Love and Death*, Woody Allen sets up a joke about an elderly man who was driven to own a piece of land and eventually holds it in his hand—a small clump of lawn. For an urbanite, the joke works; what's the difference to an apartment dweller between a handful of sod and a range of acres?

The difference, of course, is in one's heart. Hit the roads soon and head out to open space. See what it's like to get away from stoplights and deadlines. Or look about your own home and treasure it anew. Let yourself love a place. The love will be returned.

MAY 9

More sports teams are named after animals than anything else. The panther, the manta ray, and the shark lend their symbolic power to the teams; even the oriole, the blue jay, and the gopher conjure a regional pride that helps a team win for its hometown. These animals are totems.

Many people identify with a particular animal, but adopting a totem animal is different. Your totem animal is a creature whose grace, power, or mystery gives you the ability to keep going. There's no need to trudge through this world with only your own strength. Try connecting, even if only through the power of imagination, to the qualities of an animal you call sacred.

MAY 10

Where are the trees pointing?

Toward the sun? Toward the stars? Toward the sky?

Are they showing you the birds racing through the sky? The smog that hovers over your city? The pace and pressure of a world where helicopters regularly patrol your neighborhood? Perhaps they're showing you the night, with its comforting mysteries, or the day, with its honesty and heat? Perhaps they're simply pointing the way upward, out of your own preoccupations?

What are the trees telling you?

MAY 11

We know that dogs that can smell traces of evidence we could never detect and that cats can hear things we might never notice. Animals can sense storms before we can, and some say they can even predict earthquakes. They sometimes act strangely and we think they're crazy—until we understand what they perceived about the world that we did not.

You may also know people who behave oddly—but they just might be sensitive to things that are escaping your notice. Some among us have senses that are so acute that they behave in ways that confuse us. Perhaps you are one of those people yourself. Honor those who are especially attuned to the mysteries.

MAY 12

Now that spring is in full flower, it's a good time to climb a mountain. Ascending to the heights is not only good exercise, it's a spiritual practice as well. As Annie Dillard writes in *Pilgrim at Tinker Creek*, "You can heave your spirit into a mountain and the mountain will keep it, folded, and not throw it back as some creeks will . . . the mountains are home."

Resisting gravity as you hike a mountain, you recreate the structure of a life, at first loping easily but not seeing much, then trudging more slowly while enjoying the benefit of experience and a wider viewpoint. Then you get to reverse the trip, hiking back down, moving carefully so as not to let gravity pull you into a fall—all the while profiting from a new perspective on the place you left.

MAY 13

Our bodies produce a constant rhythm, which may explain why some small children and animals sleep better next to a ticking clock or metronome. Perhaps Shakespeare's poetry is so timeless partly because its iambic pentameter mimics the steady beat of our own hearts: ba-thump, ba-thump, ba-thump.

Put your ear next to someone's heart and listen to the pace of life. Listen to an animal's heartbeat sometime, and hear the amazing rush of passion and blood within, so similar to our own heartbeats and yet so different. Watch the seasons, the heartbeat of the earth.

There is music all around us, within us.

MAY 14

Climb a tree. Step out onto a balcony. Take a ride in a hot-air balloon. Take a small plane up into the skies. Soar in a jet or rocket. Then take a look below, and see how your home has changed.

Streets become lines drawn in the dirt, cars become ants, lakes become splashes of paint, and fields become lush, rich carpets.

Every place you know is transformed by your viewpoint. The troubles that plague you today look small from a distance. Joys too may shrink in size, but they become part of a greater joy, the infinity in which we live. Change your perspective.

MAY 15

Millions of people function without the use of one sense or another. People are born blind or deaf, or become so. Even the sense of taste or smell can be damaged. But imagine what it would be like to lose the sense of touch.

Touch is what allows us to both experience and differentiate ourselves from our immediate environments. Take an inventory now: What do you feel on your skin? Where? How much?

We may think of ours as a visual culture; sounds stir our hearts and our imaginations. But your skin is the primary mediator between your mind and the world. Live in it fully.

MAY 16

Some 2,600 distinct species of plant and animal life have been catalogued as living in Lake Baikal, Russia. Many of them are found nowhere else on the planet.

Perhaps your own backyard is another Lake Baikal. The biodiversity of our world is breathtaking, and more species call out for notice than we'll ever know about. Astonishment awaits us in every wild side we walk.

Creation is so prolific that it defies our imaginations. If there is an author behind it all, she never erases.

MAY 17

Many children have pet turtles, and they often create a little parkland for the creatures in their backyards, perhaps a couple of square yards surrounded by snow fencing. They may even bring it water and foliage every day, and yet still the turtle will run away, to the extent that what it does can be considered running. Even if the kids keep the turtle in a terrarium, within moments after they let it out to play, it will look to be on its way.

But the turtle may be moving toward something rather than escaping. Within a couple of blocks or a handful of miles, the turtle knows how to find a forest, a beach, a sweet stream with lush vegetation. It doesn't want to flee but to come home.

Every departure, every journey has within it the seeds of a homecoming. No matter where we are traveling, we are always on our way home.

MAY 18

The American volcano Mount St. Helens blew on this date in 1980. The devastating eruption rained ash for miles around. Yet it was not long before the natural world began working to heal the damage. As Frederick Turner writes in *Rebirth of Value: Meditations on Beauty, Ecology, Religion and Education*, "the flowers growing in the desolation of Mt. St. Helens testify to what in human beings we would call a lunatic hopefulness, the optimism of the amateur . . . Nature sends in the clowns."

Nature is perhaps the truest amateur, doing everything as if for the first time, without payment but for the sheer exhilaration of doing it. No matter the tragedy, with time the wilderness offers us hope.

MAY 19

Many of us fantasize about being able to fly. But in our dreams we eventually land and rest. Imagine birds so fast that they can simply open their mouths and feed on bugs while they keep flying, creatures so driven that they bathe, groom themselves, and collect nesting material on the wing, creatures so compulsive that they even mate in the air.

The life of the swift is hard to picture, and yet some of us perform every task on the fly. Don't forget to set down, fold your wings, and enjoy the nest every once in a while.

MAY 20

In this season of courtship, nature offers us some unsettling role models. Some animals engage in dazzling display to attract a mate while others compete with rivals in deathly contests. And some creatures don't need any contact with each other at all to reproduce.

No matter what the practices involved, all of creation seems driven to seek another, whether to procreate or simply to love. Communion is both an act of faith in the future and a celebration of the present.

MAY 21

Often we're under assault before we realize it. The spring flowers spread their aromas, and without knowing why, we're heartened, dazed, and distracted. We're delighted.

In his poem "Iris," William Carlos Williams describes searching around the house for the source of a remarkable odor: "then a blue as out of the sea struck startling us from among those trumpeting petals."

Get out of the house—get out of the city if you must, and visit a meadow, or a greenhouse, or a botanical garden, or at the very least a florist shop. Invite the assault on your senses; let yourself be pulled out of the everyday.

MAY 22

As the spring planting season comes to a close, say a prayer of gratitude for the softness of the earth. A perfectly solid and impermeable tract of land would allow no access for the plow or the trowel, no nurturing crevice or cranny for seeds to enter and take root.

The lesson applies to ourselves as well. Some of us insist on perfection and cultivate seamless exteriors, flawless emotional surfaces that attract admiration. But without allowing for imperfections and admitting weaknesses and vulnerabilities we will never grow. Like the earth, we require a certain invasion by others in order to make the most of our potential. Don't be too shiny and hard; let ideas take root inside you.

MAY 23

All animals have ways of sensing danger. Fish have a ring of scales that allows them to sense water pressure. Alive to the fluctuations in pressure around them, they can find sustenance, avoid enemies, and meet companions.

Are you gliding through the world without this advantage? What would happen if you opened up both your senses and your heart to the fluctuations in spirit all around you? Attune yourself more closely to the world, close enough to feel the silent joy that your family takes in your company, or the secret concerns that weigh down your friends' hearts.

MAY 24

Edward Abbey's remarkable book, *Desert Solitaire*, describes the severe beauty of Moab, Utah. To him it's the most beautiful place on earth, but he knows this is a personal judgment. "Every man, every woman," Abbey testifies, "carries in heart and mind the image of the ideal place, the right place, the one true home, known or unknown, actual or visionary."

What is your one true home? How far away is it from you in space, in time? Is it actual? And if it's only a vision, what would it take to make it real?

MAY 25

It's impossible to look at a lion or tiger and not think of power. We call these beasts majestic. But nature knows no social caste system. The lion is not the king of the beasts, nor is any other creature.

Too often we think of power in the terms set forth in the Old Testament, in terms of dominion. Even if we turn from the Bible to Darwin, the "survival of the fittest" paradigm suggests that nature respects only the power to kill or be killed. Yet the New Testament teaches us that love takes precedence over power—while Darwin also shows us plenty of species that survive even though their evolutionary adaptations are curious at best. What power gives the platypus its place on earth?

Perhaps there is only one true power that nature respects—and it comes from the heart.

MAY 26

The poet Rilke writes, "Whoever knew how to flower: their heart would rise above all weaker dangers and find solace in the greater one."

It's hard to think of blossoming as dangerous, but it does involve risk. As long as you're in the state of potential, the state of possibility, you haven't lost anything. Consider that you may have invested too much of your self-image in the idea that you're "promising." Take the risk of becoming something else. The world will welcome you at the peak of your powers.

MAY 27

Thomas Pakenham's book, *Meetings with Remarkable Trees*, calls our attention to the massive trees that tower over neighborhoods all over the world, each a unique goliath we have taken for granted.

"Nowhere," he writes, "are these astonishing objects to be found in more profusion than close to where millions live." Yet we tend not to appreciate the giants in our parks, beside our churches, and behind our schools until a storm or a developer has brought them down. And so Pakenham undertook to spend more time with the trees he loved—not hugging them, exactly, but finding ways to let them know he cared. There's no sense waiting for a special occasion or a calamity; cherish the arboreal beauties in your block today.

MAY 28

The next time you go to a meadow, or even your own backyard, lie down in the grass. Your instinct will be to stare up into the sky, but instead turn your gaze so that it is even with the top of the lawn.

You may be amazed at the teeming life you see. "Earth's crammed with heaven," writes Elizabeth Barrett Browning, "and every common bush afire with God." If we define God as the interdependent web of all existence in which we dwell, there's no arguing with the poet's proposition.

Life hides within leaves, under rocks, floating in the seemingly empty air. We are never alone.

MAY 29

Beautiful iridescent rings of ice and crystals orbit the planet Saturn, giving this world a distinctive place in our imaginations. But we are used to the outsider's view of Saturn—what would those rings look like viewed from the planet's surface? From many spots on the globe, they'd appear as a bright thin line bisecting the sky.

It's a startling image. We think of nature as a glorious whole, without any geometry dividing it into arbitrary lefts and rights, ins and outs. Imagine if there were a line across the ocean; it's a preposterous idea. Imagine a line across the deserts, the canyons.

And yet on our maps, we draw such lines all the time. We imagine that the earth can be bisected, subdivided into any portions we like. Let us put aside the false dichotomies that divide us, and celebrate the glory of creation in which we all share.

MAY 30

There's an unsettling moment in Jacques Perrin's otherwise inspiring documentary *Winged Migration*. A wounded seabird lands on a beach and is quickly beset by a small army of skittering, clacking crabs. A creature who soared through the skies only moments before suddenly finds itself brought low.

Respecting nature means appreciating both its beauties and its dangers. The food chain, in some ways, is a human intellectual construct. Our status at the top of the food chain is possibly temporary, and definitely open to negotiation. In any aspect of life, we are sometimes the predator and sometimes the prey. An honest appreciation of this reality may keep us not only safer—but humbler.

MAY 31

The Bible praises the faithful as the salt of the earth, and the historical value of salt is well-documented, even giving us the word *salary* for the precious salt rations that Roman soldiers received as their pay. But today, when salt seems so plentiful, we may be oblivious to its simplicity and value.

Pablo Neruda, in his "Ode to Salt," writes that salt sings a mournful song from the depths and corners of the ocean. "The smallest, miniature wave from the salt-cellar," he argues, "reveals to us more than domestic whiteness; in it, we taste infinitude."

Many people look on faith as a leap, an act of simplicity. But if the faithful really are the salt of the earth, then faith requires both flavor and depth.

June

JUNE 1

Traditionally the month of weddings, June is named for Juno, wife of the Roman god Jupiter and goddess of fertility and birth. Historically, after all the fertility ceremonies of the spring that ran from the Equinox to May Day, pregnancies started to show this month. Couples then sealed their relationship and safeguarded the life they began by marrying, whether in the Midsummer Handfasting ceremony or in more socially sanctioned Christian wedding services.

No matter what our activities of the spring, June summons us to recognize that life is in its fullness now, and to take steps to nurture and sustain that fullness. Whatever there is in your life that needs celebrating, don't be so busy planting the seeds that you're missing the blooming.

JUNE 2

Summer beckons with its visions of sand and sun. But no sandy expanse is as simple as you think. Even the Sahara, imagined by most of us as a vast wasteland of dunes, is home to some 1,600 species of plant life.

And these plants have a lot to offer. A variety of palms can produce molasses, provide writing paper, and even help dress wounds. Dates don't just offer a tasty treat; they are also a source for alcohol or syrup. And plants may sink their roots some eighty feet or so beneath the surface in search of vital water.

When resources are rare the ingenuity of life itself rises to find solutions.

JUNE 3

It's prom season and young women all over the country are shopping for silk gowns. Silk first became popular in China some five thousand years ago when the nobility's couturiers discovered that the cocoons of the silkworm could be pulled apart and spun into a remarkable cloth like nothing else on earth.

If a tiny worm can produce something as elegant and ethereal as silk, just think what you might bring forth. It takes time and care and patience for the silkworms to spin their creations, commodities that we often deny ourselves. But is time really in such short supply? Are care and patience so very hard to find? With those raw materials, the chance to weave something fabulous is at hand.

JUNE 4

Mythologies across the world feature animals who confront us with riddles. Sometimes they are familiar animals endowed with mysterious power, like the coyote trickster or Anansi the spider. Some are enigmatic hybrids, like the griffin and the sphinx. In reality there are animals whose very existence is a puzzle to science.

Consider the roles we ask these creatures to play for us, and the answers they may hold that we have forgotten.

JUNE 5

In Adrienne Rich's poem, "What Kind of Times Are These," she tells of a remarkable place in the woods, but adds that she won't explain where it is. She worries that it will be bought, harvested, destroyed, so its location must be protected. So why describe it at all? Rich answers, "In times like these, to have you listen at all, it's necessary to talk about trees."

What do you hear when somebody talks about trees? Why do they catch our attention and our imaginations?

And in order to talk to somebody about these times, what trees would you describe?

JUNE 6

Among the *Rhinoderma* frogs, a tiny species found in Chile, the males swallow the eggs of their offspring—but not to eat them. The baby frog grows and hatches inside its father's body, until one day it hops out of dad's mouth! Male seahorses also carry their gestating offspring inside a small pouch until the babies are ready to emerge fully formed into the world, and male penguins often assume the task, cradling the eggs atop their feet while their mates go foraging.

Rare though these cases may be, they suggest that nature doesn't insist on strict job descriptions for the genders. In some ways, we are all both fathers and mothers.

JUNE 7

A young boy is given an encyclopedia and starts devouring knowledge of the world. But at a certain point it overwhelms him and he turns to his mother, voicing the fear that everything will already have been discovered by the time he grows up. His mother reassures him: "Don't you worry! When you grow up there will be plenty left for you to discover."

The boy was Francis Crick, born this day in 1916. He would go on to discover (with James Watson) deoxyribonucleic acid, the DNA molecules that are the very building blocks of life. In celebration, encourage the love of discovery in young people within your circle—and never forget there is plenty left to discover.

JUNE 8

In summertime the desert calls to us. Throughout history, seers and sages have come to its expanse and left wiser than they came. The symbolist poet Juan Ramon Jimenez argues that people discover themselves amid the barren sands: "You find in solitude only what you bring to it." Environmental ethicist Susan Power Bratton, in *Christianity, Wilderness and Wildlife: The Original Desert Solitaire*, counters that pilgrims to the desert find something larger: "struggle, and contact with creation, and a place expansive enough for God to be God."

Consider what you might find in a desert where all the distractions are swept away. Will it be, as Jiminez suggests, something of what you know deep down inside yourself? Or will it be, as Bratton believes, something of what the divine knows?

JUNE 9

Decades ago the produce sections of supermarkets were tiny. Iceberg lettuce ruled, and asparagus was exotic fare. In recent years that's been changing—we can now find chard and bok choy even in chain supermarkets, although we still have to hunt a bit if we seek lemon cucumbers or striped tomatoes.

In winter a biological impulse may discourage you from experimenting with new varieties of food, the same impulse that makes us scrimp and play it safe to get through the months of cold. But the approaching summer is the perfect time to taste what you have never tasted before—in your life as well as in your salad.

JUNE 10

As the spring comes to a close and summer begins, drink to the successful completion of the season. Water, wine, or strawberry lemonade—it makes no difference; it's the drinking deep that matters.

The poet Rumi writes of spring, "We're drinking

wine, but not through the lips. We're sleeping it off, but not in bed."

Walk outside and let the air intoxicate you. Allow spring's climax to tickle its way through you.

JUNE 11

Rivers swell at this time of the year, filled not only with thawed snow but also with the power of spring thunderstorms. Beautiful but dangerous, they bear watching and can never be taken for granted.

Heraclitus teaches that you can never step into the same river twice. Time shapes us all. Nothing is constant, and nothing symbolizes flux more clearly than a river.

Build a sand castle on the riverbank, and you may be disheartened at how quickly it's washed away. But it's not destroyed; the elements of your work are simply sent to new destinations. And even as the river takes from you to feed the world downstream, it's bringing you new material from upstream.

JUNE 12

When *Esquire* interviewed basketball player Shawn Bradley of the Dallas Mavericks, the reporter asked him what it's like to be so tall. At seven feet, six inches, Bradley sees a world the rest of us rarely glimpse. The surprising thing is that he sees a lot of dust—on the tops of lockers and refrigerators, even on the tops of the molding in people's houses.

We often wonder about what it would be like to see through the eyes of somebody taller, shorter, or stronger, or something fiercer or faster or even airborne, like bears and cats and eagles. Yet every person and every creature may wonder the same thing as well; their viewpoints have drawbacks as well as assets. Consider the things that you see, both good and bad, that nothing else in nature sees.

JUNE 13

The word *ecology*, only recently coined, comes from *eco*, meaning home, and *logos*, which may mean knowledge, science, or even the verbal magic with which God instigated Genesis. When we focus on ecology, we are dwelling on the magic of our home.

Walk around your own home and ask yourself how well you know it. Do you know how the plants on your balcony yearn toward the sun? Do you understand the community of trees that give you shade? Do you value the magic of the mud in which your children play?

What ecology do you create?

JUNE 14

When you see a hummingbird across the garden it seems silent. Get close enough, though, and you'll hear the steady whir of its amazing wings. In the open air, the throbbing dissipates gently, but in a contained space like a porch, the beating of hummingbird wings can sound like a miniature dive-bomber.

Sometimes in order to hear or see truly we must set up the right conditions. A tree seems to alter its shape with the glare of the sun behind it. Rainbows appear and disappear as you shift your position. Don't ever assume you see the world as it is. Adjust your position and discover how things change.

JUNE 15

The sun is with us more and more each day, culminating in the approaching solstice. In the comic books, Superman is powered by the sun, specifically by solar radiation that floods his cells with special energies. But it's not just any sun that sustains the first superhero—it has to be a yellow sun. The fictional sun of his home planet is red, and in its rays he's powerless.

The allegory suggests that super-strength is something that comes from where you are in the world, and that it can grow as you travel to new places. Staying in your own neighborhood may be comforting, but try venturing out into forests, lakes, and mountains you have never seen before. Under their sun you may feel more powerful than a locomotive.

JUNE 16

In elementary school the solar system was presented to us as a series of shimmering orbs, and the easiest one to remember was always Saturn because of its rings. But it turns out that many planets have rings. Now that the night sky is clearing from the clouds of winter, the rings of Jupiter, Uranus, or Neptune may be visible through a telescope. Even here on Earth, the Moon orbits in a reliable ring about us.

Any sizable mass will exert a gravitational pull upon moons, ice, or other debris that drags them into its orbit to form a ring. Similarly, we are all encircled by a small galaxy of acquaintances, friends, and family members who draw in and out of our orbits, sometimes apparently vanishing for years at a time only to circle back into view when we least expect them. We are never alone; there are rings around us all.

JUNE 17

Joy Harjo's poem, "She Had Some Horses," offers a dreamlike catalogue of beasts. "She had horses who were bodies of sand . . . she had horses who laughed too much . . ." After indexing all the horses of her life—the crazy ones, the manic-brave ones, the shy ones, and the quiet ones who have created their own solitude—Harjo reveals they are all the same.

These horses lurk within us all. Ancient cultures worshipped horses as wild and primal creatures capable of reconnecting us with the roots of the world. Yet they are also among the most gentle and docile of creatures, some of our steadiest partners on the planet. When you look into a horse's eyes you may see something of your own wildness—or your own docility. Can you own both?

JUNE 18

Annie Dillard writes that "nature's silence is its one remark." Sharman Apt Russell counters that sentiment in her book, *Anatomy of a Rose: Exploring the Secret Life of Flowers*: "Nature has never been silent for me . . . Nature whispers, and sometimes shouts, 'Beauty, beauty, beauty, beauty!'"

In Russell's account of the floral kingdom, she also observes that a single flower can produce a wealth of chemical compounds, some of which even detoxify both land and water. The flower's beauty goes even deeper than we know; that which is truly beautiful is that which heals and nurtures the earth.

JUNE 19

All planets have a magnetic sphere, which means they broadcast on wavelengths that can be picked up by radio equipment. Jupiter, the largest of the planets, sings so strongly that even the government takes note. The Federal Communications Commission has created a "quiet zone" so that amateur hobbyists can listen to Jupiter's song on their home radio equipment.

Earth, of course, has its song as well, and we are all part of it. When you sing your own song, know that it's just one element of a harmony. The vibrations echo back and forth between you and everyone, everything you know. You're a part of earthsong, which keeps reverberating through you—even when you feel you're performing a solo.

JUNE 20

The holiday that begins tonight is generally known as "Midsummer," even though popular understanding considers early August to be the middle of summer. The early Celts divided the year into summer and winter— which makes today the midpoint of that six-month summer. It's a historic time for mischief and tomfoolery— a time when Shakespeare imagined young lovers leaving the city and being beguiled by the magic living in the wilderness. The adventures of the Bard's characters on Midsummer Night were so wild that they had to be dismissed as dreams—but unlike dreams, they would be remembered forever.

The long months ahead will shine brightly enough— tonight, with the mystery of darkness shorter than on any other night, prize the magic that may await you.

JUNE 21

During this, the longest day of the year, the sun lingers like a guest who doesn't know when to leave, but we're happy to entertain him as long as possible. In some far northern cities the skies stay light until eleven at night. And in Point Barrow, Alaska, the sun never sets at all tonight.

With sunlight running a marathon today, it's a day for clarity. The midsummer madness of night can be set aside for a clear look at the landscape around us. Nightfall's passions are in abeyance, so perhaps we can find a different kind of passion—the white heat we feel in seeing things as they truly are.

JUNE 22

A popular theory claims that the mysterious rocks of Stonehenge in the English countryside form a natural calendar, but that theory has been debunked of late—which means that the mystery of the henge remains.

Henges, the constructions of banks and ditches that mark off an area for some sacred or ceremonial purpose, can be found in a number of sites throughout England. We may never know their exact purpose, but perhaps we don't need to. The wonder of a setting like Stonehenge is that it reconnects us to the mysteries of the earth, to the inexplicability of stone, the implacability of the earth. Here long before us, here long after us, the substance of Stonehenge reminds us to be humble—in both the spiritual and the earthly senses of the word.

JUNE 23

Whack! Out of nowhere, the unlucky hiker discovers he's just had his ear pecked by a magpie. These birds are ferociously territorial and may well swoop down upon an unwitting trespasser venturing too near to their nests, even though the trespasser may mean no harm to its children. Schoolchildren in Australia have even been known to wear metal buckets on their walk to school in order to stave off a magpie attack.

We are sometimes just as territorial as the magpie. Do you attack sometimes out of instinct, without considering the full situation? Define your territory as the world, and there will no longer be intruders, only valued and necessary companions.

JUNE 24

Magnetic fields. Ultraviolet rays. Microwaves. It's crowded out there in the ether, jam-packed with all kinds of phenomena we rarely notice.

The wife of physicist Andrei Sakharov told a story in which someone asked the famous scientist what he loved most. She figured he'd say something sweet about her or their family. But Sakharov's affection for them notwithstanding, what he loved at that moment was background radiation emanating through the universe, the almost undetectable hum that still reverberates from the big bang. He loved it as a phenomenon that tantalizes us with the possibility that everything really does fit together in this universe.

Many things we love prove the same point—even our families.

JUNE 25

Clearly, getting hit by lightning is a bad idea. Yet from time to time people survive it. Gretel Ehrlich, in her memoir, *A Match to the Heart*, describes getting hit by lightning twice and living to tell the tale. After one of her lightning-strikes, she woke up to the face of Robert Redford, who'd been in the area filming a movie, and believed for a moment that she might be in Heaven!

Our own hearts, of course, are filled with a kind of electricity. Static electricity flows around our skin and through our hair on occasion. And then there's that certain spark that flies between two people when their spirits are truly open. Whitman sang of the body electric, and we are all part of the current.

JUNE 26

Many people have never seen a cicada, while others have seen all too many of them. They're rare in much of the country, appearing only at intervals ranging from seven to seventeen years. But other folks are familiar with the mysterious, trilling locusts that spring up out of the earth. For them, the harsh song of the cicadas is one of the classic refrains of summer.

When the cicadas go to sleep and wake years later, they encounter a different world, but they don't perceive the changes. Instinctually, they come out into the air, mate, and die exactly as their parents did during the last breeding cycle. Likewise, we go to sleep each night and wake the next morning, often with no real recognition of a new day beginning. This morning, look around you. What is different today?

JUNE 27

Today is the birthday of Helen Keller, the philosopher and teacher who changed our perception of what it means to be blind and deaf. Keller listened to the radio by putting her fingers to the box and feeling the vibrations, just as she rested her hand against a singer's throat to hear his voice.

Music is grounded in touch. Our ear drums are designed to register small, invisible vibrations as sound. And the converse is also true: Touch is music.

Let your fingers rest against the ground, amidst a pet's fur, along a child's hair. Pay attention to textures, temperatures, resistance, and pliability. You hold a symphony in your hands.

JUNE 28

In these balmy summer days, some say there are two types of people—ocean people and pool people. Some need to connect with the wildness of a beach, the infinity of the sea, while others prefer to bask in the simplicity of a pool, practicing their dives and perfecting their strokes in its symmetrical safety.

Either way, we give great thought to how we might swim more strongly, more gracefully. If our behavior in the ocean can be so thoughtful and playful at the same time, so can our behavior on firm land. You can run through the park or tumble among the waves with the same sense of abandon. The world is your home whether wet or dry.

JUNE 29

Swimmers and divers at this time of the year enjoy the richness and color of coral reefs. But coral is no accident; it only grows under very specific conditions. The water in which it thrives must be saltwater, not freshwater, neither too dirty nor excessively muddy. And while it rarely grows above the surface, neither can it grow too deep, for it requires regular infusions of sunlight in order to photosynthesize food.

Once those stringent conditions are met, however, coral is one of the natural sculptors of the world, unleashing a cornucopia of remarkable colors and shapes. There is plenty of accidental beauty in the world; some of the rarest beauties require time, care, and rigor to reach their full flower.

JUNE 30

Joanna Stratton writes in *Pioneer Women: Voices From the Kansas Frontier*: "Set against the stark terrain, the summer storm was a dazzling spectacle with its violent claps of thunder and brilliant flashes of lightning. Yet this beauty was deceptive." Sudden floods could overwhelm the land and hailstones could wipe out a harvest.

From a distance, nature often looks gracious and generous. Yet up close, we can be equally astonished by its relentlessness, even its cruelty. Humanity is no different. It's easy to love humanity as an abstraction, but up close it's harder to ignore people's flaws, their stubbornness and cruelty. Just like nature, we all carry gifts and flaws. Can you embrace them both as part of creation?

July

JULY 1

Today is the midpoint of the year on Western calendars. But of course there are many other calendars, the marking of time being a human obsession, and while our own calendar has been arranged for the purposes of clear administration and honoring Roman and Norse deities, other calendars have separate purposes entirely.

The Aztec calendar, for example, divides the year into months ruled over by different gods, so that each god has a fair crack at ordering the universe in her or his way. As explained in Kay Almere Read's *Time and Sacrifice in the Aztec Cosmos*, the Aztecs saw time and nature as living in precarious balance. Each god warred with others to tip the balance, so, to keep the war at bay, the calendar assigned each period of the year to a different deity. Perhaps as we enter this month, rather than tip our own balance with our long list of duties, we should assign certain tasks to this time alone. To everything, after all, there is a season. What will you devote your next season to?

JULY 2

On the Kola Peninsula in northern Russia there's a hole in the earth that's over seven miles deep and was created specifically to enhance our understanding of the earth. Now the deepest well in the planet, the Kola project has drilled some 40,000 feet into the ground. And even at this, it's still only scratching the surface (literally), exposing for scientists the mysteries of the earth's crust. Researches will have to dig many more miles to reach the planet's mantle.

Some superstitious people fear that we're digging either into Hell or into a lost subterranean civilization. Maybe that's how we know the work is important—after all, Galileo's study of the natural world violated long-held superstitions and changed our understanding of the universe. Let us remain open to the chance that it could happen again.

JULY 3

In Norse mythology, the worldtree Yggdrasil holds the universe together. With its roots in the soil, its trunk solidly on the ground and its branches in the stars, it bridges all creation and remains a striking symbol of our interconnectedness.

Many traditions see the heaven and the earth as clearly separate realms, but our urge to unite the two spheres runs deep, represented in the Biblical story of the Tower of Babel as well as modern edifices such as the Sears Tower and the Transamerica Pyramid. Perhaps the more we believe that heaven is reachable from earth, the more we will believe that anyone can get there.

JULY 4

Fireworks were one of the first manifestations of the sublime. When they were first introduced to the courts of Europe, the explosions evinced a certain terror in the spectator, terror that quickly became awe at the beauty of the pyrotechnics. Just as there is an alchemy among elements that creates glorious explosions, there is an alchemy in our souls that can do the same thing.

As fireworks explode tonight, consider the natural chemistry at work—both in the skies and in your heart.

JULY 5

Today is our planet's aphelion, the day on which we are farthest from the Sun. On other worlds, aphelion might be a day of freezing catastrophes, but the unique combination of our planet's gravity, circular orbit, and rotational speed keeps us safe.

Still, scientific theory says that the universe is expanding, and on this day we may be sensitive to the vast differences that separate us, not only from other worlds but even from each other. Overburdened schedules, too many commitments, and time-saving devices that actually speed up the pace of life all conspire to pull us apart from each other.

From this day forward Earth edges closer to the Sun every second. Perhaps today we should begin edging closer to the sources of warmth in our own life.

JULY 6

Monarch butterflies practice a startling kind of self-defense. They feed frequently upon milkweed, a poisonous plant. It doesn't kill the monarchs, but it does fill their bodies with poison, making them risky snacks for birds and other predators—one bite and the attacker will learn the monarchs are better left alone.

Sometimes we poison our own wells so that nobody will try to take what we have. What toxins are you storing up? Do they really serve you?

JULY 7

Ritual cleansing dates back centuries, most famously in the practice of John the Baptist. You can create your own ritual cleansing. In her book *Soapmaking: A Magickal Guide*, Alicia Grosso not only guides her readers in the making of natural soaps from vegetable oils and herbs but even discusses how the soaps can be infused with wishes, dreams, and prayers.

Your own body can play a role in your spiritual practice. Western thought has spent much time and energy divorcing the spirit from the physical, but in using art to cleanse yourself, you honor the temple of your body—and give extra force to its dreams.

JULY 8

As much as Ringo Starr might want to take us to an octopus's garden, in real life we'd be reluctant to go. Still, octopi and their cousins, the squid, are enviable for many reasons. Every parent has wished she had as many limbs as these sea creatures boast. Their eyesight is remarkable, with capacities to distinguish light that we simply lack. They are fast; squid in particular easily outpace other creatures. And they are fierce, even successfully fighting off sperm whales who seek them out as food.

These creatures evolved this remarkable array of skills under pressure and in the dark. When stress increases in your own life, you may not grow extra limbs to cope. But you can develop your spirit in unexpected new ways.

JULY 9

The wildfire season is upon us. Uncontrolled flames are deeply unsettling to us all, but elk, moose, and many other species depend on fire to give them open ranges, and the forests themselves often thrive once they've burned up excess fuel. There are even some species of trees that require the intense heat in order to reproduce.

Perhaps God spoke to Moses through a burning bush for a reason, just as Prometheus risked terrible punishment to bring fire to humanity. In the energy that a blaze unleashes, radical transformation happens. Mastering the flame is one way we define ourselves as humans, and perhaps a way in which we touch the divine.

JULY 10

On particularly bad days, when your job seems oppressive and you have to fight through endless traffic jams to get home, you may head inside and snap, "It's a jungle out there!" But of course, if it were really a jungle, you'd have to worry about hippo-induced fatalities.

The mammal responsible for the most human deaths in the African jungle is not the elephant, the panther, or even the lion. Hippopotami, for all their plumpness and seeming tranquility, are highly aggressive if they sense a threat. And given that they can run up to eighteen miles per hour, you can't escape them if you get their dander up.

No creature should be underestimated. Within even the tamest animal or person is unexpected strength that can be dangerous and yet inspiring.

JULY 11

The next time you're at the ocean look for starfish, called sea stars by scientists because they have no actual relationship to fish. Starfish are famous for their regenerative properties, the way they can regrow a leg if they lose one (or even three). They're less well known for another startling trait—they can change gender at will.

Starfish remind one of Ursula K. LeGuin's historic science fiction novel, *The Left Hand of Darkness*, which argues that gender is not a dichotomy but a continuum. Her characters on the planet Winter modulate between male and female extremes, in a fashion deeply disconcerting to travelers from planets with the typical two sexes. Interestingly enough, while nations on Winter certainly have their harsh rivalries, they never conduct wars. Perhaps the starfish and the characters in LeGuin's book share a message: If we can accept that there is a little bit of male and female in everyone, we can heal ourselves.

JULY 12

Pearls are formed through irritation. When an oyster is bothered by a grain of sand, pebble, or bacterium, it exudes a secretion to coat the offending particle. That secretion grows and solidifies into beauty so rare and lovely that divers risk their lives for it.

Think about the irritations in your own life. Can you create beauty out of them?

JULY 13

Willa Cather's poem, "I Sought the Wood in Summer," tells of its protagonist despairing during the hot months. The trees tremble beautifully in the light, the daffodils glisten, yet every breath Beauty "gives the vagrant summer but swifter woos her death." It's not until the poet returns to the wood in winter that she sees the power of beauty, its ability to renew itself continually.

Amid the season's heat and light, it's easy sometimes to forget there has ever been or will ever be anything else. But we cannot judge a thing by the climate of one day, or even one month. It's not until you spend years in a place that you know its true strengths and weaknesses, the range of its miracles.

JULY 14

In the summer heat many people cut their hair to help them cope with the temperature. But these shearings can be dramatic events for some people, a wrestling with their self-image. Long, thick, wavy hair has an undeniable power, power so threatening to some that it was demonized in the image of Medusa, who had snakes for hair. Shorter hair has a different kind of power, making a subliminal statement that its wearer has conquered physicality. Athletes and warriors cut their hair to symbolize their discipline as much as for any practical reason.

As you shape and style your hair, your most flexible feature, think about what messages you are sending to yourself and others. Hair reminds us on a daily basis that no matter how proud we are of our intellect, we remain creatures of nature.

JULY 15

These days schoolchildren all learn about continental drift. One only has to look at a globe for half a minute to understand this theory, to see how South America might fit inside Africa's curve, how Australia might have nestled next to India.

But geophysicists are creating theories even more dramatic. The theory of the supercontinent cycle argues that the breakup of a supercontinent into many smaller masses wasn't a one-time thing. Instead, this theory advances the unsettling notion that the planet's land masses keep joining and then separating. Perhaps, hundreds of millennia from now, the continents will merge again to form one giant territory.

Clearly stubbornness can always be overcome; no matter how intractable a situation may appear, over the long haul even the continents themselves shift their positions.

JULY 16

In July, writes the Korean poet Yi Yuksa, blue grapes are blossoming: "Village wisdom clusters around the vines, the distant skies enter into each berry."

With every bite we take we are digesting more than mere food. We are partaking of an entire culture that produced that food—its colors, its smells, its gossip, its truths. And we are sharing in the wealth of the whole world, even the rains that fed our food, the sun that infused it with energy, and the winds that shaped and caressed it as it grew.

Eat wisely. Eat well.

JULY 17

Summer swimming changes us like no other sport. We're suspended amidst the depths, buoyed up as we have never been since leaving the womb. Diving into an environment in which we can't breathe, we demonstrate how alive we are. And when we leave the water, refreshed and exhilarated, it's so similar to being born again that it's no wonder baptism speaks so powerfully to people.

Woody Allen's character in *The Front* explains to a woman he's courting, "Swimming isn't a sport, swimming is what you do so you shouldn't drown." But maybe swimming saves our lives in more ways than one. Perhaps this form of recreation literally allows us to re-create our very selves.

JULY 18

Today is the birthday of one of Sir Isaac Newton's contemporaries, Robert Hooke, who is little remembered today outside of the scientific community. But Hooke, an inventor, architect, and physicist, was among the first to inspect the natural world with magnifying lenses. His description of the composition of cork gave us the word *cell.* He had the remarkable imagination to believe that there were truths in nature that his eyes could not see. Hooke and his colleagues had the openness of spirit to suspect there was more to this world than had been dreamt of in their philosophies.

Keep your eyes open—look deep and look close. Things are nearly always more complex than they appear at first glance, and the deepest truths may be invisible ones.

JULY 19

If you have ever witnessed the birth of a human being or an animal, you know how breathtaking, alarming, and transformative the moment can be. But birth is often precarious and although we're used to thinking that a newborn is a small, delicate thing, many baby animals are able to walk on their own within moments of entering the world.

Birth is a kind of explosion, an incredible release of energy. The newborn may be frail, or it may be bursting with vitality and stamina, awaiting only time to come into its full strength. The birth may be a girl or boy, a wild creature, a soul newly awakened, or an idea that will change the world.

There are newborns every day. Honor their power.

JULY 20

Imagine a desert the size of the United States. You're imagining the Sahara.

Large enough that it spans eleven countries, the Sahara seems a boundless arid wasteland. Yet there is evidence that thousands and thousands of years ago, the land on which the Sahara now sits was home to forests and elephants.

Nothing, in other words, is eternal. Nature is our expert witness that all things must pass. Even though no joy is forever, neither is any pain. Live in them both fully while they are here.

JULY 21

Flamingos dance—and we have no idea why. It could be a mating ritual or a survival mechanism. They may not even be having fun.

We do know that flamingos live off algae, which means they're not in competition with nearby animals for their food, that they can drink remarkable amounts of water within mere seconds, and that they evolved to survive conditions of extreme heat. But as for the dancing, maybe it's best left a mystery. When you're dancing, you don't really want someone asking why you're doing it. Maybe it's time just to cut a rug—and if people ask why, refer them to the flamingo.

JULY 22

Laurel Olson writes, "I will dig my fingers into the soil and remember what it is that sustains me."

The things that sustain you may be hidden. They may grow slowly, deep beneath the surface, or they may be starved for lack of nutrients.

People think of the roots of their lives as fixed, while their lives keep growing toward the sun. But roots keep growing, too, in unexpected ways and directions. Your past may well appear different today or tomorrow than it did yesterday. Your story changes as you grow and learn new truths about yourself. Even as your wings set you free, make sure that you keep track of the myriad, changing ways in which your roots keep you grounded.

JULY 23

Few places match our dreams of paradise like the windswept, beautiful island of Hawaii. Yet when the volcanos of Hawaii erupt, lava spills over the cool, green land at about two thousand degrees Fahrenheit, scorching everything it touches.

You may know people who seem as serene and easy as Hawaii but smolder with unexpected fires deep within. Perhaps they are consumed by rage or inflamed with a passion for justice. What burns within you? Should you fan the embers or allow the flame to burn out?

JULY 24

In Robert Macfarlane's *Mountains of the Mind*, he describes how even a passing knowledge of geology broadens his idea of himself. Seeing the passage of eons among the strata demonstrates the vast scale of both time and space of which we all are a part.

While it may be daunting to measure yourself against the seeming infinities of geologic time, "you are also rewarded," McFarland argues, "with the realization that . . . unlikely as it may seem, you do exist."

Turn the common feeling of being dwarfed by the planet on its head; dwell instead on the idea that you are included in the grandeur of creation.

JULY 25

Deep in the Amazon lives a tribe called the Mayoruna. They adorn their noses with thin reeds that resemble the whiskers of felines. Facial tattooing adds to their catlike appearance. As Petru Popescu explains in his book *Amazon Beaming*, the Mayoruna partake of the power of jungle cats through such rituals.

The panther, the leopard, and the tiger inspire us with their elegance, their economy of movement. In silent determination they survey the landscape and move only when the wind is with them. When they play, no creature plays harder, but when the time for play is over, no creature is more intense. The next time a black cat crosses your path, consider it good luck. He's reminding you that he has family who can offer you help.

JULY 26

Out in the desert century plants are growing. Certain cacti, agave, and yucca plants grow extremely slowly for many, many years (not always a real century) before they ever bloom. For those raised in wetter climates where the rose bush blooms several times over the year, this may be a startling concept. But it also means we should revise our ideas about blossoming.

Contrary to popular mythology, not everything blooms in spring, nor does everything bloom when you expect it.

Your own great blossoming may be yet to come.

JULY 27

Our bodies are about seven-tenths water—and so is our planet.

Perhaps, then, we're more physically in touch with the earth than we generally think. Go to the ocean, the lake, even just the creek down the street, and run your hands through the substance that gave birth to all life on the planet and nurtures you still.

In these summer days when water seems so valuable, consider its fluid ease, its cleanliness, and its simplicity. All you have to do is look inside yourself to go with the flow.

JULY 28

Spend a day on the seashore, and you can watch the tides all day as they make tiny, meaningless changes in the sand. Come back a season later, and the changes won't seem so meaningless. A sandbar may have appeared—or a whole section of beach may have been swept away to China.

If, in the words of Ghandi, we must be the change we seek to create, then often we must work in small strokes. The big picture may not even come in clearly until we've been at it for a while. But tide after tide, nature is our ally in reminding us that there's nothing that can't be accomplished if we can find that strange combination of softness and inexorability that we admire in the ocean.

JULY 29

Snakes are famous for shedding their skin, a trait that contributes to their unfortunate reputation as duplicitous creatures. But it's a brilliant adaptive mechanism, so brilliant that we engage in a version of the same practice ourselves.

Our own skin is constantly replacing itself, too. The process isn't as dramatic as the serpent's, but we are constantly leaving behind our old skin and presenting a fresh face to the world—both literally and metaphorically. What part of yourself are you ready to discard? Can you renew your spirit by casting off some old idea that has died and no longer serves you?

JULY 30

In science fiction adventures, strange plants often menace the heroes. Whether it's *Lost in Space*, *Day of the Triffids*, or *Invasion of the Body Snatchers*, the slide-rule types who star in these stories don't know what to make of the vegetation, the pods and flowers that take away their power to reason.

Walk through a greenhouse or an arboretum and your senses may be swept away, immersed in the limitless invention of our mother earth. We may learn more from the green than we do from the lab—at least our spirits may.

JULY 31

Antlers are remarkable biological phenomena. Unlike horns, which are composed of keratin and grow permanently, antlers are made of bone and shed every year, only to grow again.

In difficult times we grow our own defenses. We cultivate a facade that warns people: Don't mess with me. When the battles are over, though, our facades sometimes stay in place, making it hard for people to connect with us.

Are you holding onto any defenses that you no longer need? Wisdom means knowing when to defend yourself and when to make room for new growth.

August

AUGUST 1

The pagans call this day Lammas—from ancient words meaning "loaf mass," for on this day today the ancients baked the first loaves of the harvest. This is only the beginning of the season, the full harvest is yet to come. But the crops we have sown, the plans we have laid, have now borne enough fruit that we can sample their richness. For the first time in many months, the corn and the wheat can be gathered up into the bread of life.

The old holiday carol "Winter Wonderland" urges us to "face unafraid the plans that we've made." But in the earth cycle, the real time for facing your plans is not wintertime, but now. How are things growing? Do you have enough resources to nourish you through the cold months ahead? Or do you need to tend your fields more deliberately? Celebrate this day for what you've achieved thus far, even as you mind the future.

AUGUST 2

Because of the seasonal habits of our ancestors, the school year will be starting soon. Perhaps you are leaving home for a campus near or far. Or maybe your children (or these days, even your parents) are flying from the nest to take up their studies. Either way, the air is seasoned with both expectation and wistfulness. We often look forward to the discovery of knowledge, the intellectual excitement of the learning community—but gaining knowledge can also mean losing innocence.

Summer heat warms, but it also ages. Take a moment today to appreciate the paradox.

AUGUST 3

If you're hot today and in need of water, there's more than one way to get it. You can go to the store or the river or the faucet. Or you can dowse. Dowsing is the ancient art of finding water (or occasionally metals) by tuning in to your own electromagnetic sense.

No one really knows how dowsing works. Yet with the use of a dowsing rod to magnify their perceptions, skilled dowsers have been able to locate unsuspected riches in the earth. Maybe it's just luck. Or maybe this ability comes from another source; consider that dowsing is also called divining.

How do you know where to look for the nourishment you seek? Maybe it's divine guidance, or maybe you can tap into the divine within yourself.

AUGUST 4

"My own position changes," writes Thomas Moore in *Care of the Soul*, "when I grant the world its soul."

On this kind of summer day, when the earth feels spread open before you like a feast, take time to consider that the world may indeed have a soul. If so, then it's more than a vast treasure trove of resources and more than a heritage whose stewardship we have been given. It is a life force with its own gifts of expression, a life force that acts on its will just as we do.

We're often told to think of the earth as our home, but how many of us never clean our homes? Try instead to think of the earth as your soulful companion.

AUGUST 5

"Of what avail are forty freedoms without a blank spot on the map?" asks environmentalist Aldo Leopold. How far would you have to travel to find someplace outside the vision of civilization? And what would it be worth to you?

While this isn't an exhortation to "get lost," there's something a little sad about always knowing where you are. If you've lost your bearings it can be unsettling, even life-endangering. But for some people, it can also be exhilarating. You're never in touch with your surroundings as much as you are when you're lost. Every tree tells a story that you never heard before and every shadow offers a clue. Whether you are lost in nature or lost in your own work, think of it as an opportunity to act, to define yourself and your world, that isn't offered to those who stay only on the beaten paths.

AUGUST 6

As we solemnly mark today's anniversary of the Hiroshima bombing, it is heartening to note that the most enduring symbol of healing is a symbol from nature. Centuries ago, Japanese civilization began venerating the crane, and the image of a thousand cranes became common in artwork. The crane was known for long life, and origami cranes became a gift to wish each other health and well-being.

Some cultures also believe that cranes pray every morning. Perhaps whenever we focus on nature, we are praying as well. Prayer is intentionality and resolve, strengthened when its roots run deep in the earth.

AUGUST 7

At this time of year the summer air can be oppressive, sapping our energy and weighing us down. Perhaps it's trying to tell us something.

In this labor-driven, multi-tasking society, it sounds like heresy to suggest that we pull back a little bit. But in these days a lot of sound and fury on our parts may well signify nothing. Perhaps we truly can accomplish more by doing less—by heeding the message in the August wind.

AUGUST 8

Our culture often frowns on crying, seeing it as weakness or a loss of control. But tears, like all water, cleanse and purify. When our faces are wet with tears we have been baptized in a way—a natural baptism, sometimes performed for us without our even asking.

And our tears also contain the salt of the ocean. In a time of sadness, our bodies will not let us forget our ancient origins. Let tears flow when they must—they are the touch of the great mother, from whom we all sprang when the world was young.

AUGUST 9

In Farley Mowat's *Never Cry Wolf*, he describes himself as a child wandering about the creek near his grandmother's house one summer. Fascinated by gasping catfish in a stagnant pool, tenaciously clinging to life, he brings them home for further study, inadvertently terrifying his grandmother, who didn't expect to find live animals swimming in her toilet.

Mowat sees clearly the seed that was planted that day: "The affair of the catfish marked the beginning of my career first as a naturalist, then as a biologist." Any child exploring the wild on a day like today could be in for a similar transformation. Discoveries and decisions await you. What will you find today?

AUGUST 10

Long before we discovered longitude, centuries before the invention of the compass or the sextant, Polynesian navigators regularly crossed the Pacific Ocean with nothing to guide them but their eyes and their imaginations. Being awake at sunrise was critical, as was watching the exact direction of the sun and the nature of the waves, studying sunsets and memorizing the movements of hundreds of stars.

Today it's hard to imagine drifting in the middle of the ocean with no maps or navigational clues. But if you dedicate yourself to reading the earth you need never be lost.

AUGUST 11

In *Thoreau as Spiritual Guide*, Barry Andrews observes, "It seems a little odd that Thoreau would begin his book on life in the woods with a chapter called 'Economy.'" But certainly anyone living as far from any neighbors as Thoreau did on Walden Pond would be painstakingly aware of his resources and how they were deployed. A life lived close to nature requires a daily inventory of usable materials.

Such economy may not come quickly to some of us, accustomed as we are to the rhythm of getting and spending. But as Andrews reminds us, Thoreau points the way when he writes, "To maintain one's self on this earth is not a hardship but a pastime, if we will live simply and wisely." What do you have to work with? Do you make the best use of both your inner and outer resources?

AUGUST 12

"I discovered in nature," writes Vladimir Nabokov, "the non-utilitarian delights that I sought in art." To some critics, Nabokov's fondness for examples of natural life that seem to serve no evolutionary purpose means that he believes in a divine Creator. Traits he found in butterflies and leaves appeared so random that they seemed to him like the stylistic flourishes of an Author. But what we think is random may only seem so because we're too close. Like the individual dots in a pointillist painting seen up-close, the details of our lives and the world around us may appear meaningless, but someone standing further back from the image can see how every dot contributes to the greater whole.

The further you travel both in time and distance, the more you can see the patterns underlying all nature.

AUGUST 13

Thunderstorms are one of the highlights of summer. But they're a rare event in many parts of the country. If you're pining for thunderstorms and can't see them, you may be able to hear them. Lightning generates a kind of music, called *sferics*, which you can sample if you tune your radio to empty frequencies. More sophisticated radio equipment can pick up the sferics of auroras and magnetic storms.

When people talk of the music of the spheres they're not just being poetic. Vibrations travel all around us, and the more you listen, the more you become a part of the vibrations yourself.

AUGUST 14

Have we lost our vocabulary for nature? The characters of Jane Austen, Thomas Hardy, and the Brontë sisters used to frolic in copses and fens. They'd intrigue in the sward or dally in the swale. They'd forage in the weld until they came across an interesting tarn. No croft or stile or weir could keep them from enjoying a mere or a dale.

Today we probably have more words to describe styles of homes than we do for the architecture of valleys and lakes. Today, leave home and develop a new vocabulary of wonder.

AUGUST 15

Some two centuries ago at about this time of year, American explorers Meriwether Lewis and William Clark discovered that the greatest danger they faced in their expedition might be themselves. Lewis took a bullet in the buttocks when one of his companions accidentally fired his gun during a hunt. In his journal entry for that day, Lewis complained that he could not keep writing because the pain was too intense, but he felt compelled to comment on the minutiae of nature: "I must notice a singular Cherry which is found in the Missouri in the bottom lands . . ."

How many of your varied little aches might be alleviated, even if only for a moment, by the sight of a beautiful tree or a powerful river? When you feel you can't keep going turn your attention to the natural world around you.

AUGUST 16

Does the caterpillar know what's about to happen when it spins a cocoon? Does it realize that it's doing more than simply seeking safety? Does it understand that it's involved in something greater than simply acting on instinct? Does it imagine, within its long-sought rest, the beauty to which it will open itself? Does it glimpse the possibility that it may continue its life in a dramatically different fashion than anything it has experienced up to this time?

Does it have any idea that it's about to transform?

Do you?

AUGUST 17

"We are stardust, we are golden," writes Joni Mitchell, "and we've got to get ourselves back to the garden."

Her song "Woodstock" endures not because it memorializes the rock festival held on this date in 1969 but because it speaks to the human condition. We *are* stardust; cosmic matter from the fires of creation lingers in each of us. We *are* golden; not only are we literally filled with minerals but their combination within us is as rare as any gem or precious metal. And murmuring within many creation myths is the idea that we emanated from a pristine source of nature, the garden.

Tap into the heavens, the precious treasure, and the thriving life within yourself.

AUGUST 18

Dig a trench, delve into the earth, and sooner or later you'll come up against roots.

Roots take all manner of shapes; some are thin as strings, others are plump and juicy enough to eat. They meander in all sorts of directions, wrapping themselves around obstacles, gnarling in all directions to anchor themselves in the soil. Many people think of roots as the stalwart and unchanging bases of trees or plants, but roots continue to expand and grow just as the visible part of the plant does.

What about your own roots? What have they gnarled around? Do you need to sink them deeper in search of sustenance?

AUGUST 19

"Before you can learn the trees," writes poet Howard Nemerov, "you have to learn the language of the trees." The quaint and varied vocabulary of botany is a forest in itself, and with each leaf you study, you learn more about *serration* and *venation*. After enough time, you can name them like Adam, describing them by genus and phylum. Yet the more you study, the more you realize that words are poor constructs to sum up the wonder and individuality of any given tree.

Indeed, learning the language of the trees may teach you more about language than it will about trees. And the final lesson may be that the heartwood of any given tree is ultimately unlearnable. What the trees know, they keep to themselves.

AUGUST 20

Imagine that you are a tourist on your way through the southwest United States and you stop to admire the Painted Desert in Arizona. You stand on the edge of an overlook, drinking in the colors of the earth, thankful for the glory that nature has provided, when suddenly something moves in your peripheral vision. You glance sideways to discover a huge spider cresting your shoulder.

What do you do now? Perhaps you yelp and jump, contorting yourself to make sure it falls far away—in the process losing your balance, sliding down the slope a good thirty feet before you come to a stop, nearly becoming part of the Painted Desert yourself.

Are you more comfortable with nature at a distance? What boundaries do you maintain between yourself and nature? At what proximity can you really accept the world?

AUGUST 21

Marianne Williamson's *Illuminated Prayers* includes this petition: "Please bless the sapphire globe and the diamonds on the water."

We humans tend to value precious gems most when they are pulled out of nature, when they're polished and their facets gleam with that special man-made brilliance. We're never content to leave sapphires and diamonds where they are.

Yet maybe if we treat the earth as though every grain of it is precious, if we treat the ocean as we would a sparkling array of gems, then it will no longer need God's blessing, for we will have blessed the earth ourselves with our adoring.

AUGUST 22

Today is the birth date of Claude Debussy, the classical French composer who forged a new style in music, leaving behind the percussive qualities of the piano to create sinuous, intricately woven melodies. His delicate, impressionistic pieces were deeply influenced by nature.

Listen to "Clair de Lune," "Gardens in the Rain" or "The Sea." The piano work in these pieces is like the rain or the moonlight itself: gentle, fluid, working almost invisibly. When we listen to music like this, we are reminded that in our everyday lives, nature is a subtle force, insistent and yet patient, comfortable but also quietly passionate. You don't have to spend a night on Bald

Mountain to delight in the musicality of the earth.

AUGUST 23

Things may be cluttered, askew, a sordid mess. Oh, maybe they're not that bad . . . they're just a little sloppy. Nonetheless, you've been hard on yourself for not getting everything done or cleaned perfectly.

Take a moment tonight and look up at the stars. How orderly are they, really? We try to impose order by drawing them into constellations, but that's a vain and futile effort. Part of what makes the heavens so spectacular is their chaos; as Edmund Burke writes, "The apparent disorder augments the grandeur, for the appearance of care is highly contrary to our idea of magnificence."

Perhaps just for today, let the chaos be. Embrace magnificence.

AUGUST 24

The word *touchstone*, which we often use today to mean a specific standard of quality or authenticity, actually refers to a black siliceous stone that produces colored streaks when rubbed with gold or silver. These streaks are indications of the metal's purity.

Basalt or jasper are frequent touchstones. It's striking that we judge the purity, and thus the value, of precious metals using a substance as gritty and substantial as they come. Perhaps our standards of worth should always come from the inarguable realities we find in the earth.

AUGUST 25

Onions don't get much respect. Back in the sixties, radios played a novelty song about a girl who loved onions; her back-up singers sang "Yuk! Yuk! Yuk!"

But the humble onion wasn't always so disparaged. "I will not move my armies without onions," warned General Ulysses Grant. And long before that, Herodotus tells us that the onion was so prized that slaves working on the pyramids staged a small revolt when they were denied their rations of the vegetable.

Indeed, the Egyptians considered the plant holy. Its many layers matched their vision of the cosmos—the earth surrounded by the atmosphere surrounded by the heavens.

No food, no plant, and no person can be understood at first glance. There are always layers within layers.

AUGUST 26

Bushmen of the Kalahari sleep on the ground, listening to what lies ahead, behind, and around them. The closer we get to the earth, the more we know.

Have you ever investigated the ground on which your house sits? Where it sits in the flood plain? What soils, what waters, what winds surround you?

If you love the earth, get dirt on your hands. If you love the oceans, get wet. If you love the sky, breathe deeply.

AUGUST 27

These late-August weeks are called the "dog days." And not because it's so hot that you see sleeping or panting canines everywhere you go, but rather because the ancient Romans saw the Dog Star prominent in the heavens during this month. But our own lives are so distanced from the constellations that the expression connects us instead to the actual dogs in our lives.

Dogs, cats, and animals of all varieties keep us grounded in the moment. A dog barking to go out or begging at the dinner table isn't thinking about tomorrow. Perhaps even better, as Walt Whitman said of animals, "They do not make me sick discussing their duty to God." Maybe they don't need to; maybe the more time we spend amidst the animal kingdom, the more God's presence feels evident.

AUGUST 28

"Speak to the earth," says the Book of Job, "and it will teach thee." All things are known to and made by God, Job tells us.

Some of us do speak to the earth and learn proof of God's hand in everything, while others speak to the earth and learn more about the divinity of their own hearts. Still others speak to the earth and learn that the earth itself is God.

What will you say to the earth? What is it you wish to learn?

AUGUST 29

"Solitude is a human presumption," writes Barbara Kingsolver in the closing passages of *Prodigal Summer*. "Every quiet step is thunder to beetle life underneath."

Ray Bradbury visited this same theme in his story, "A Sound of Thunder," in which a time-traveler's casual damage to a butterfly changes the course of time itself. We are connected to everything and everyone through invisible threads, and our actions tug at those threads whether or not we choose to know it. The next time you stroll out into the summer sun think about what you are changing—perhaps for the worse, perhaps for the better. With each passing moment, how are you changed?

AUGUST 30

The Trinity River outside Dallas, Texas, has seen better days. But as John Buehrens explains in *A Chosen Faith*, appearance isn't everything. When Buehrens remarks to his colleague Jacob Trapp that the shallow, tainted water is not unlike the tainted shallowness of the worst Bible Belt revivalists, he is calmly corrected. Trapp calls his attention to the small signs of beauty in the river and reminds his friend that in New Mexico, "the river came from life-giving springs, easy to forget but capable of cooling and refreshing the soul, even on the hottest, harshest day."

Buehrens urges us to resist despair, for if we voyage back to the springs, we can reconnect with the source, with the purity that made us love in the first place.

AUGUST 31

About this time of year, as Rodgers and Hammerstein put it, the corn is as high as an elephant's eye. Walk into a cornfield and you're in a living labyrinth grown from the earth. In such a maze, you can get so turned around that it can take you hours to complete the short trip back—for some an unsettling experience, for others an exhilarating puzzle.

Some fairs have gone one step further and created their own corn mazes for visitors' enjoyment. Some spiritual seekers create their own labyrinths with stones. In these homemade mazes, getting to the end isn't the issue. Rather, you're urged to watch yourself as you walk the maze, for the way in which you decide on your path will teach you something about the way you walk through life.

Whether we're making our way through cornstalks or stones, we are all searching.

September

SEPTEMBER 1

September is the best month for viewing the Milky Way, although some see it clearly as early as July. Get out of the city or the suburbs and into the countryside, away from light pollution; if you've never taken in the sky like this, you may be astonished to see the cloudy white smudge that is our galaxy.

The Swedes refer to the Milky Way as the "winter street"—but *milk* and *winter* are simply words to describe its brilliant whiteness. The words *way* and *street* suggest a pathway awaiting us. The stars beckon. Maybe if we travel that street, we will come to a place where we no longer consider ourselves the only creatures in the universe. For centuries the Milky Way was thought to comprise all of creation, but the farther we look down the path, the more wonders we find. Celebrate the limitlessness of creation—a street that never ends.

SEPTEMBER 2

Late August and September are the months when berries ripen and bears come out foraging. They're not looking for trouble, and when they hear you coming, they're glad to disappear. But silent and solitary hikers and mountain bikers don't give the bears any warning. Travel in pairs or groups as you explore, letting your conversation warn the bears that they have company.

So often we think of adventuring as a solo task; there's a great romance to the image of the solitary figure trekking through the woods. But working with allies makes our lives safer and fuller—not only in the wilderness but in all the paths of life.

SEPTEMBER 3

One of the most striking sculptures in history is Bernini's rendering of Apollo and Daphne. According to Ovid, the lustful Apollo pursued Daphne, who pleaded with the kinder, gentler elements of the Greek pantheon for deliverance. Her prayer was answered—she was turned into a laurel tree. This might seem a terrifying transformation, yet there's an undeniable beauty in Bernini's sculpture, in Daphne's gradual metamorphosis. Leaves grow from her fingers, roots from her feet, and it's not monstrous but poetic. Imagine Daphne's relief as she grows strong, rooted, far removed from her fears.

Bernini's art demonstrates that the closer we grow to nature, the more peace, beauty, and strength we may find. Keep transforming yourself, growing close to the world that offers you roots.

SEPTEMBER 4

School's starting, and kids are still asked to write about "what they did on their summer vacation." What did you do this summer? Has it occurred to you that it might still be worth writing down?

Keeping a journal can focus your eye on nature in a new way. How many toadstools grew in that far corner of the yard? What color were the finches that sang this morning? How long did it take to hike that trail, and how long did you stay motionless while the doe stared back at you?

You never know something as well as you do when you have to write about it. If you want to strengthen your contact with the wild, create a personal record of it all. Words, photographs, and drawings can all immortalize passing, transient beauty.

SEPTEMBER 5

At some zoos and fairs, you can ride on the back of a baby elephant. It's a fascinating experience, feeling the leathery, hairy skin of the pachyderm. It's also a glancing contact with another world, a world that will always be separate.

In his wide-ranging *Guns, Germs and Steel*, Jared Diamond points out that while we think we have tamed elephants, they remain undomesticated. "Hannibal's elephants were, and Asian work elephants are, just wild elephants that were captured and tamed; they were not bred in captivity." Many species such as elephants simply will not mate in captivity; they resist efforts to bring their entire existence under our sway. Let us respect that there are some creatures whom we may never fully understand.

SEPTEMBER 6

Perhaps one of the most profound expressions of nature is the simple equation $E=mc^2$. Einstein's calculation establishes that every mass contains a remarkable quantity of energy.

Look around at the common objects in your room. Every object—even a bookmark, a paperweight, or a pair of shoes—contains enough power within itself to light a sun. And you are no different. What will it take to release the energy inside you? You might shed light across distances you've never dreamed of.

SEPTEMBER 7

As the autumn approaches and the foliage begins to change color, consider color itself. A red leaf is arguably everything but red, because red is the only color that it reflects, while it absorbs the rest of the hues in the spectrum. Perhaps this has implications for racists, who might consider that they actually absorb every color except the one they proclaim themselves to be. Certainly it has ramifications for any astute observer of the world: Nothing is as simple as it appears.

If we are to see anything in its "true colors," we should consider all the colors we think it's not.

SEPTEMBER 8

Michael Pollan argues in *The Botany of Desire* that plants have domesticated us as much as we have domesticated them. "They got us to settle down, start farming, cut down trees all over the world so they could have more habitat," Pollan explains. "It makes just as much sense to look at the adventure of agriculture as something that the grasses did to us as we to them."

The idea may sound like something out of science fiction, but we acknowledge the idea that flowers attract insects to pollinate them, so it's not inconceivable that they attract us as well. We consider ourselves part of the interdependent web of all existence; with the imminent harvest, perhaps we should work on thinking of ourselves as *just* a part, rather than the dominant part.

SEPTEMBER 9

This season is enriched by the celebration of the Jewish New Year, Rosh Hashanah. It's a fitting time to reflect on the meaning of the word *Shalom*. Though often translated as *peace*, in the fuller sense of the word, *shalom* literally means *wholeness*.

When you wish people "shalom," you're wishing them a fuller sense of themselves, a reconnection with nature, or a sense of renewed harmony with the world around them.

We are, sadly, rarely in perfect harmony with the cosmos. But when we dwell on the ways in which we fall short, let this time urge us to seek connection anew.

SEPTEMBER 10

It's apple-picking season, and with the innocent pleasures of apple pie and cider awaiting, it's hard to imagine that apples were involved in the Bible's first and worst calamity. Then again, the apple's status as the forbidden fruit is frequently challenged. Many people draw on botany, archaeology, and linguistics to argue that the serpent tempted Eve with an apricot, a tomato, a fig, an orange, a pomegranate, or even a banana.

In her thoughtful volume, *Reinventing Eve*, Kim Chernin relates the story of the Hawaiian queen Kaahumanu, who overturned native taboos on what women can eat by consuming a forbidden banana during a court ceremony. Seen in this light, Chernin argues, Eve is not the weak link in Genesis, but a heroine of disobedience. Could we make this fall's harvest a ritual celebration of the fall itself?

SEPTEMBER 11

These are the weeks that are best for harvesting honey. Consider the life of the beekeeper, nurturing nature's most efficient go-betweens, even as he knows that he'll be stung if he fails to show them proper respect. In September apiaries cull the sweetest honey of the year, while taking care to leave enough in the hives so that the insects will weather the relatively flowerless months ahead. Russian poet Anna Akhmatova writes, "Wild honey smells of freedom." Taste a bit of honey and appreciate the industry and instinct that go into it—both from the bees and from the beekeeper.

SEPTEMBER 12

Wilderness paths quickly deteriorate without careful maintenance. The growth of summer brush, when followed by rains and snow, may swallow up some courses so thoroughly that no trace of their existence is left.

Now is the time, then, for a little tending of the trails, not only in our parks, forests, and mountains but in our own social spheres as well. Ahead is an increasingly demanding work schedule, followed by a gauntlet of holidays. Amidst all the craziness, don't let the pathways, the delicate trails that connect you to what you care about, become overgrown. Take the time to tend to them now, so that you can find your way when you really need to.

SEPTEMBER 13

You're longing to do something about your garden, but it will be months until spring. But you don't have to wait. It takes a little more cleverness to garden in the fall, to look for plants with strong roots and give them the chance to get a start before true winter comes. But the savvy horticulturist will realize that all nursery supplies and accessories are actually on sale during the fall, and you have your pick without all the competing crowds of springtime.

Don't let others dictate the seasons of your life. Look at your habits and consider whether you hold onto them because they're common practice or because they suit you best.

SEPTEMBER 14

The leaves are turning and change is in the air. In many locales seasonal changes are dramatic and unmistakable. But those who live in arid climates like Los Angeles or Tucson commonly say there are no seasons there.

In such places you need to be mindful and patient to see the clear differences between winter and spring and between summer and fall. Change, the only constant, is everywhere around us.

As the palette of nature changes and the fall colors grow more intense, embrace your own changes. That which does not change is not fully alive. As humans in chaos, we sometimes long for stability, but flux and ongoing evolution bring us to our fullest selves. In the words of Carl Jung, "Only that which changes remains true."

SEPTEMBER 15

As winter is associated with northern winds, spring paired with the eastern sunrise, and summer linked to southern breezes, so the coming autumn is tied to the west. Look to the sunset, to the tranquil Pacific, and relax in the cool and the quiet.

Consider what rituals can make the autumn welcome for you. Make apple butter. Take a hayride. Gather the falling leaves and knit them into wreaths.

Call on friends too long neglected. Light candles, join with a group of elders, and read out loud from John Keats's "To Autumn." As befits the fall, honor maturity.

SEPTEMBER 16

The Jewish day of atonement, Yom Kippur, includes a reading of the Book of Jonah. We know little about Jonah save that he was called to preach to Nineveh, ran away instead, and was eaten by a whale. It is his adventure in the belly of the beast that calls him to our attention.

Perhaps Jonah, tiny and anonymous at the beginning of his story, was thrown into the whale's maw not for punishment but for growth. By surviving inside earth's mightiest creature, he gained the personal strength he needed to carry out his mission. Such an encounter with the profound power of the planet might have been the best thing that could have happened to him—inspiring him with the power to endure anything.

SEPTEMBER 17

Try to draw an eagle. Take a pencil and shape wings, the beak, the limber yet strong torso.

Then be patient as you tear up the drawing and try again—and again and again.

No picture can ever capture the full majesty of the bird. The trick is not to get caught up in trying to recreate nature—an impossible task!—but rather to put your childlike wonder about flight into the effort. We cannot equal the marvels of the world, but our feelings about them can be marvels in themselves.

SEPTEMBER 18

In his collection *Season Songs*, the poet Ted Hughes makes a September cranefly into a character from a romance, desperately escaping one peril after another, with only occasional respites from the drama of her life: "Sometimes she rests long minutes in the grass forest like a fairytale hero."

The questing never ends. Ants struggle desperately to complete their missions. Worms wrestle their way onward like miners in the darkness. Far above, birds joust and court frantically as if time is running out.

Perhaps every bird, every bug, every one of us on God's earth is a kind of hero. Celebrate the small victories you achieved today.

SEPTEMBER 19

As the leaves turn colors, perhaps you are inspired. Or you may be saddened by the trees' final blaze of glory before the year reaches its end. Mikhail Gorbachev once said, "Trees are my temples and forests are my cathedrals." The holy spaces are now bedecked in festival decor.

The September trees provide us with a special sanctuary. The riot of color shows us that a holy place need not be severe, and the array of wildlife demonstrates that sacred ground need not be silent or solemn.

The divine is wherever you say it is.

SEPTEMBER 20

As fall approaches, people sometimes worry about aging. They regard their wrinkles and laugh lines, and bemoan the loss of their younger faces.

In nature, of course, old things are beautiful. Weathered stone has an authentic attraction that competes well with polished gems, and a young cactus looks pitiful next to its mature and majestic neighbor. Virgin forests appear too fragile to disturb, while many long to walk among the aged sequoias.

Autumn is part of the process of nature, both in our world and in ourselves.

SEPTEMBER 21

Ervin Drake's "It Was A Very Good Year," relies on the metaphor of the harvest. The singer looks back on his seventeenth year, his twenty-first year, his thirty-fifth year, judging each one as he would taste grapes stored away for wine. And then he's done! After he's thirty-five, the last verse puts him in "the autumn of his years." Is it all just dregs once you're thirty-six? These days, life is just starting to ripen at age thirty-five. Don't harvest the grapes until you really feel ready.

SEPTEMBER 22

One task of the autumn equinox is reckoning. How do our stores stand as we face the winter? Are we prepared for the weather to come? Summer has been a time of ease, of lazing in the heat, but now we must plan for the shorter and colder days ahead.

It's tempting to romanticize Nature, but the world doesn't automatically provide us with everything we need. It takes planning, the endless nurturing of seeds and dreams, and the hard work of a timely harvest to help us through the winter.

Harvest is an opportunity to practice mindfulness. Whether we chop wood and carry water, or whether we reap the investments we've placed into careers or families—the growing chill in the autumn air reconnects us to the now and prepares us for the season ahead.

SEPTEMBER 23

Autumn is the time of maturity. Native American tribes look to Mudjekeewis, the spirit of the west wind, to inspire them. In Henry Wadsworth Longfellow's poem "Hiawatha," the north wind is too cruel, the east wind is too young, and the south wind is too lazy and languid. It's the west wind that inspires the hero, that leads him to conquer evil.

Our culture, obsessed with celebrating youth, may not have a full appreciation for what the autumn teaches us. But today, take a look outside, at the sun that finds a deeper place in the sky, at the leaves that take on more distinctive personalities. Quietly take it all in, and be thankful for the lessons that time has brought into your own life.

As you grow more mature, taste both the bitter and the sweet. You have been seasoned, and your life is richer for it.

SEPTEMBER 24

"I am haunted by waters," says Norman Maclean in his novel *A River Runs Through It*. Perhaps because their work is the slow accumulation of detail and image, novelists seem especially sensitive to rivers. "Riverrun" is the first word of James Joyce's masterpiece *Finnegan's Wake*, Mark Twain's most beloved classics owe their existence to a river, and Philip José Farmer's science fiction saga, *Riverworld*, depicts all souls in the afterlife united on a vast river.

The work of a river often resembles our own work, seeking small things, carrying them onward, and depositing them on the shore when it's time, until the current brings everything into the larger world. Perhaps your work is like that of a river as well. The skills of the river—patience, strength, grace, flexibility, poetry—may be the same skills that you bring to your own calling.

SEPTEMBER 25

Ostriches are demeaned as hiding their heads in the sand. It's a slander, for they're actually searching for food, craning their necks so that they can graze. When their tiny heads vanish behind the landscape, however, it can certainly look as though they are hiding.

But ostriches are actually remarkably powerful. Ostrich wranglers don't let naive visitors too close to the birds, for their claws can do serious damage if they feel threatened.

Appearances can deceive. The silliest and strangest among us have unexpected capacities.

SEPTEMBER 26

There are giants traveling this world, but we pay no attention to them. Deep beneath the waves, dwarfing every other species, whales circle the globe.

How is it that we are not more familiar with them? As Jeff Poniewaz writes, "If ancient Egyptians worshipped cats, how much more should we worship whales!"

But then, the world is full of wonders we have neglected, in our fretting and frenzy. What wonder is calling out for your acquaintance? Listen.

SEPTEMBER 27

In his poem "There Was a Child Went Forth," part of the *Autumn Rivulets* cycle, Walt Whitman describes the things that a child sees in his daily wanderings—the shadows, the field-sprouts, the wharves and the ferries, the clouds and the apple trees, the workers, and the families both kind and cruel.

He closes with a startling image: "These became part of that child who went forth every day, and who now goes, and will always go forth every day."

Are you like that child who never stops adventuring? What is becoming part of that child within you? Are you incorporating shadows and fieldsprouts, workers and wharves—or malls and plastics, televisions and technologies? Today is your chance to let nature become part of you.

SEPTEMBER 28

Today museums devote whole exhibits to the study of butterflies, but it wasn't so long ago that collecting them was an unthinkable practice. Butterflies were considered meaningless and about as worth collecting as lint. Sharman Apt Russell, in *An Obsession with Butterflies*, tells us that the first woman to collect butterflies was judged legally insane because of her hobby.

Is there some facet of nature that fascinates you more than any other? Do your family and friends find your fixation peculiar? Persevere. Perhaps you are discovering something that will mean as much to the rest of us one day as the inspiration we find in a butterfly taking wing.

SEPTEMBER 29

"Gold autumn's joy," writes Pushkin, "oblong, transparent, like the slim fingers of a girl." He is talking about grapes.

Ever since the "Song of Solomon" was written, it's been clear that food not only nourishes our bodies but reconnects us to our physicality. It's no surprise to anyone who has seen the astonishingly sensual photographs of peppers created by Edward Weston.

As fruits and grains reach their fullness in this season, they call us back to ourselves, to the passion that drives forward the human race. Take in the textures, soft, meaty, or pliant. Take in the rich smells, the intoxication of tastes. Live when you eat.

SEPTEMBER 30

Some people look at the leaves falling and grow melancholy at time's passing. This can be a melancholy time of year. And yet, nothing's more fun for a group of children than to rake a huge pile of leaves and dive into it again and again, spiraling and plunging and catapulting their way through the afternoon.

How much do you let your environment shape your mood? The next time the sight of something "makes" you sad, resolve to see it differently. If you can respond creatively and positively to the changes taking place all around you, you may be able to recapture the spirit of childhood.

October

OCTOBER 1

Although June is famous for weddings, agrarian societies once traditionally celebrated marriages in the fall and winter after the harvest was in because there was too much work to do in the summer months.

Perhaps it makes more sense to marry in the fall, so that couples can weather the cold winter months together. But whether or not you're in a marrying time, harvest is a season of culmination. The efforts of the past months are beginning to pay off, and now is the time for rest and celebration. Today, at least, rest on your laurels.

OCTOBER 2

Despite all of the amazing creatures that dwell on our earth, we insist on creating more from our imaginations— the centaur, the unicorn, the manticore, the griffin, and the basilisk to name just a few. Usually these beasts seem like the product of a mix-and-match game, with one trait from column A and two traits from column B, yielding something that could never sustain itself in nature. Yet their hold on our imagination remains persistent. Even moralist Christians of the Dark Ages, who discouraged theatre and other imaginative arts, wove tapestries of unicorns and griffins, constructing symbolic roles for these mixed-up creatures in the struggles of Christ and the church.

Maybe our minds feel drawn to these chimeras because they represent the boundless potential of nature. Nothing is more flexible than creation, and all things do seem possible. Perhaps when we enjoy images of dragons or winged horses, we are celebrating the thrilling unpredictability of creation itself.

OCTOBER 3

The harvest season brings with it more than the rich yield of springtime planting. It brings also the memories of the plans that were laid, the spring ambitions, the easy summer heat. Reaping is the delivery of the year's promise, and part of that bounty is the recollection of all that has gone into the growing.

David Mas Masumoto, in his memoir *Harvest Son*, looks back on the fields sown by his ancestors and carries the saga back even further. "Every year, as I work that vineyard," he concludes, "a grandson has stories to remember." As you take part in this year's harvest, stretch your mind back not only through your own life but through the lives of those who first believed in the earth and whose traditions we carry on today.

OCTOBER 4

Today many people observe the Feast of Saint Francis of Assisi, who is beloved far outside the bounds of his denomination as the patron saint of ecology. The legends about Saint Francis are like fairy stories—tales of birds that come to nestle on his shoulders and of ravenous wolves that are calmed by his presence and reform their bloodthirsty ways.

There's something in human nature that makes us want to believe in such miracles. The bond between nature and Francis of Assisi is something many of us long to experience. Edward O. Wilson called it "biophilia"— that which draws life to life. It is an innate inclination in all living things. Open your shutters and feel it today.

OCTOBER 5

The Unitarian Universalist hymn, "I Walk the Unfrequented Road," is a meditation on autumn, the season of the harvest, and the nature of harvest itself. "I gather where I did not sow," writes Frederick Hosmer, "and bind the mystic sheaf, the amber air, the river's flow, the rustle of the leaf."

All nature, we are taught, is a harvest for us, one that we did not plant but that offers itself unstintingly nevertheless. And though we may not think of ourselves as literally "bringing in the sheaves," every walk through the woods is a reaping of delicious experience. Maybe midterm exams are coming, maybe there's office work to complete before Halloween, but you do yourself injustice in spending too much time at the desk. Take pleasure in the bounty of the world.

OCTOBER 6

The fantasy writer Ray Bradbury loves this month. In his collection of stories *The October Country*, he describes the land of the book's title as "where the hills are fog and the rivers are mist; where noons go quickly, dusks and twilights linger, and midnights stay."

Mystery envelops us at this time of year, and in Bradbury's work mystery is inextricably bound to the land. Unlike so much fantasy and science fiction, *The October Country* is not haunted by dystopias or nightmare visions of technology gone awry; in another of Bradbury's books, the villain is defeated by a mere smile. Perhaps Bradbury's optimism remains unconquered because he keeps in touch with that part of him that is still a young boy, walking through the fog and mist, enchanted by the magic of midnight.

What natural vista is the landscape of your childhood? Return there in your imagination, if only for today. What fantasy calls out to you from that hopeful place?

OCTOBER 7

The second Monday in October is designated as Thanksgiving Day in Canada. This tradition stretches back far further than the Pilgrims' Thanksgiving, hearkening back to a harvest feast held in the wilderness by explorer Martin Frobisher in the sixteenth century. Thanksgiving falls earlier in Canada because the weather is so cold that the crops must be brought in before November.

Perhaps the timing of the harvest is more subjective than we think. In the southern hemisphere, of course, the time of cornucopia was six months ago. And some plans you're making right now may not come to fruition for months, even years. We observe harvest celebrations in the fall, thanks to our ancient ties to the land—but in the coming year, whenever your schemes finally bear fruit, remember that your victory party is itself a harvest.

OCTOBER 8

The trees are preparing themselves for a time of scarcity. In the months to come, they will receive less sunlight, less water. In order to survive this drought, they must strip down to their bones, choking off their leaves so that the starved blossoms turn orange and red before finally falling to the ground.

Yet we find beauty in this practice. Our wealth-based society often views privation as unattractive, but the trees, cutting themselves back for the winter, call to us so powerfully that many people plan their vacations around the sight. As you enter times of distress, look for something of beauty, something to admire, in casting aside that which is non-essential.

OCTOBER 9

French composer Camille Saint-Saens was born on this day in 1835. A lover of the natural world, he created the collection of short pieces entitled *Carnival of the*

Animals. Its themes include "The Lion," "The Swan," "The Aquarium," "The Donkeys," "The Tortoise," and even "Fossils."

You may be far away from a zoo or a jungle, and yet you can visit one through the music of Saint-Saens. Perhaps all music is our attempt to reach out to the wilderness, to mimic its strengths, its cries, its passions. In the prowling tread of a lion, in the sinuous swirl of a school of fish, there is melody. We are creatures of nature ourselves. Listen closely to discover the music of your own life.

OCTOBER 10

When there is so much real work to do on behalf of the earth, taking a camera and playing shutterbug in the meadows or canyons may seem self-indulgent. But master photographer Eliot Porter argued that photography can be "a weapon for the defense of the environment." Every snapshot carries forth a legacy and inspires those whose lives are more insulated from nature.

Porter inspired a revolution in how we see the world. Where other photographers captured the landscape, the vista, the distant peak and valley, Porter's camera got down into the detail. His brother Fairfield writes of his work, "There is no subject and background, every corner is alive." This is the cosmos' view, of course, and none is more democratic. When we walk into the woods we count only for as much as we are.

OCTOBER 11

Children think every spider is a black widow. The name is so dramatic, and the excitement of danger is irresistible. But while black widows occasionally do pop up from the woodwork, most spiders are helping, ridding houses of other, more alarming pests. And the spider, emblem of this season, is considered wise in some cultures, a trickster in others, and lucky in still others. E. B. White's great spider heroine Charlotte relies on how little we understand spiders to save her friend's life.

The next spider you see may have lessons for you—about patience, about craft, and most of all, about the power of a small creature to weave a home for itself anywhere.

OCTOBER 12

Today some people celebrate Columbus Day, while others use the day to honor indigenous peoples. In either case, the occasion reminds us of the times when America was a pristine land, whose denizens treasured connection with the earth. The oldest cultural tradition of our land sees nature not as a background for human industry but as our living companion. "We did not weave the web of life," said the Suquamish chief Seattle, "we are merely a strand in it."

Stay quiet and attune your feelings, and you may sense the vibrations from other strands of the web. You may even sense your own strand—quivering with potential.

OCTOBER 13

"Thy woods," sings Edna St. Vincent Millay to the world, "this autumn day, that ache and sag and all but cry with color! . . . World! World, I cannot get thee close enough!"

None of us can ever "get the world close enough." For all that we linger in valleys or dive into the ocean, our preoccupations keep us always a little distant.

But don't stop trying. Perhaps you cannot ever get the world close enough—yet it remains a steadfast beacon.

OCTOBER 14

Bradley Denton's novel *Lunatics* imagines that the goddess of the moon comes down to make love to an ordinary heartsick man who's been staring at her for too long. Ultimately the Moon goddess must return to her celestial enclave, but not before the man and all of his friends have learned more about their personal lunacies than they wanted to.

What is it about the Moon that drives us crazy? Do legends of lycanthropy have their roots in something real? We have traveled to the Moon, but we still don't understand it. Or perhaps we dare not understand it fully. If we lost the opportunity to go a little crazy every four weeks or so, maybe we'd really lose a lot more. Partake of a little lunacy; it could be good for you.

OCTOBER 15

Walk out and sing in the autumn woods. Sing "Autumn Leaves." Sing "Shine On, Harvest Moon." Sing your college football fight song. Or just sing random plain notes that don't necessarily add up to anything.

Listen to how your voice bounces off the bark, loses itself in the leaves. Saint Augustine writes, "He who sings, prays twice." Singing draws on a different part of your brain, a different physicality inside you. Oliver Sacks tells of a man with a brain injury who couldn't recognize ordinary objects unless there was music playing. Before it gets too cold outside to take a deep breath, share your own melody with the world. If the lark and the nightingale can do it, so can you.

OCTOBER 16

Sunset is a time of discernment.

We spend all day in the light of the indiscriminate sun, which shines equally on everything. Look above and the sky is blue, a calming, static blue. But at sunset, the rays of light that spread throughout our atmosphere are filtered in different ways. The egalitarian blue light doesn't make it across the horizon when the sun is descending. Other highlights of the spectrum travel further—brilliant reds, sensual oranges, luxuriant purples.

All these colors are present with us throughout the day, but it is only as the day ends that we can perceive them in their complete glory. Look to the ends of things and you will see them in their full splendor.

OCTOBER 17

The nights are getting longer, and as Halloween approaches their romance grows as well. Some find a special solace in the night, a comfort that eclipses the harsh world they know in daytime. Loren Eiseley's memoir *The Night Country* describes that solace, even as he warns that it is not for everyone.

"If you cannot bear the silence and darkness," he writes, "do not go there; if you dislike black night and yawning chasms, never make them your profession." Yet he knows that there are some who will find allure in midnight, energy in the ebony landscape. Eiseley sees himself and his fellow insomniacs knitting the world back together every night while others sleep peacefully. If you belong to the daytime, honor those who keep the world on its course at night—and if you belong in the night country, honor those who return the world to you every evening.

OCTOBER 18

Fireflies. Angler fish. Trilobites. Many creatures emit their own light. And the more these beings dwell in darkness, the more they evolve to illuminate their surroundings.

Do you give off light yourself? Give yourself credit. You may have a glow that doesn't register on the visible spectrum, but one that makes a difference nonetheless.

Train your eye to take in the radiance that everyone gives forth. Train yourself to recognize the ways in which you yourself light up the landscape.

OCTOBER 19

When we were young, cemeteries had a special fascination, especially at this time of the year with Halloween just around the corner. Would these deserted graveyards become partying spots for the undead? Perhaps—or perhaps not, with the gravestones remaining as stern and silent sentinels.

Consider how, while bodies return to the dust under the earth, a fragment of earth that does not decay quickly stands as a silent witness. The stones keep their shape and message for decades if not centuries.

Every living creature faces the reality of its own end, but the earth comforts us with its constancy.

OCTOBER 20

The apples are ripe now, and their names have histories as rich as the apples themselves—Granny Smith, Delicious, Empire, and Gala. The name *Delicious* was decided upon long before the first such apple was grown. It had been selected as a marketing device and held in reserve until, after many journeys through orchards, after many tastes and trials, an apple that really deserved the title was identified.

Maybe we should adopt this strategy ourselves.

Maybe the Delicious apple only appears when we've decided that's what we're looking for. To find the delicious, to live in joy, to breathe in peace—whatever our goal, we may taste many sour apples in search of it. But the more dedicated we are to the search, the more likely it is that nature will provide.

OCTOBER 21

The most modest of creatures offer their own particular wisdom. The Scots poet Robert Burns finds his teacher in a mouse.

Having overturned the mouse's nest with his plow, Burns writes to the mouse of the calamities that befall them both: "The best-laid plans o' mice an men gang aft a-gley, an lea'e us nought but grief and pain." Still, Burns envies the mouse for its ability to stay in the present, while he worries about the past and fears the future. This special genius of animals eludes us so often—but the more we remain true to the immediate moment, the less power grief and pain can have over us.

OCTOBER 22

On this day in 1734, Daniel Boone was born. John Mack Faragher's biography of the woodsman describes how, in the early years of his marriage, Boone would disappear into the forest for long hunts, sometimes lasting a year or so. After one of these hunts, Boone returned to find a child born to his wife, a child fathered out of her loneliness and his absence. To his credit, Boone accepted the child as his own and she grew to be the most loyal of children.

Hunting and trapping on the frontier, risky as it is, was probably easier for Boone than living in society. The call of the wild is powerful and ignored at one's peril—yet those who turn to the wild to escape life's complexities may find that their lives remain just as complicated upon their return. The wilderness is not an escape, but an inspiration that can make each day richer no matter where you are.

OCTOBER 23

Today the horoscope enters the sign of Scorpio, the scorpion. On one level, horoscopes are little more than a game. What makes us think that, because the ascendant constellation vaguely resembled the outline of a scorpion to the people of millennia ago, people born this month can be as selfish and lethal as scorpions? Why would Pisceans be fluid and Librans justice-loving, based on the fantasies of ancient peoples staring at star patterns? Patterns are subjective—what if they'd seen a dove instead of a scorpion?

Yet the human instinct to find meaning in nature is undeniable. And perhaps, by identifying with the stories in the stars, we become more who we are. Maybe a love of justice is nurtured by the constellation Libra, or a healthy self-esteem encouraged by Taurus. As long as there are no constellations named "rapacious corrupt deceiver," there are worse fates than to draw our inspirations from the heavens.

OCTOBER 24

Testosterone peaks in many men during the fall, and scientists speculate that we have evolved this way so that babies would be born in the easier summer months.

Testosterone is blamed for a lot of masculine excess, but women also produce testosterone, and we'd all be worse off without it. The radio program *This American Life* once told the story of a man who was deprived of the hormone for several weeks. His sense of humor changed, his voice changed, even his appetites changed. Spicy food turned him off; the most stimulating foods he could handle were Wonder Bread and mayonnaise. Motivation itself was a problem; without testosterone, everything seemed vaguely pleasant, but nothing itself seemed important enough to do.

Desire forms our personalities far more than many like to admit. You must own your desires if you are to master them.

OCTOBER 25

Creatures of the night, bats are part and parcel of Halloween lore. But they're fascinating in their own right, teaching us lessons we might not expect from such humble sources. A bat's legs, for example, aren't actually strong enough to hold it up. But bats have evolved so that they're always either flying or hanging upside down—showing us that an apparent handicap can become something we never notice. Bats use echolocation to navigate, emitting tiny sounds that orient them in the dark—teaching us to speak up to keep ourselves safe. And they hear those sounds with ears that dwarf the rest of their features—demonstrating how easily and exquisitely we can attune ourselves to our environment.

People talk about being "as blind as a bat"—but there are more ways of seeing than we generally acknowledge.

OCTOBER 26

With trick-or-treaters on their way, you yourself may be contemplating a funny, scary, or outrageous costume. Masquerade is a chance to try out alternate selves or styles that you might feel too timid to wear in your everyday life. Laws once forbade the wearing of fabrics deemed extravagant or the consumption of foods deemed too luxurious. Imagine being forbidden to wear silk, carry a parasol against the sun, or serve roast meat at a wedding feast.

Halloween offers a chance to experiment, to try out new clothes and foods—to tamper with the unconscious rules that have bound you until now. Break your laws.

OCTOBER 27

The whole idea of buying candy in preparation for Halloween may rub us the wrong way sometimes. Why should this day, which began as a harvest festival and a day upon which to show our reverence for the dead, be co-opted by confectioners?

And yet, by staying home and offering treats to visitors, we see neighbors to whom we haven't spoken for months. Friendships will be rekindled, and new ones may even begin. In his essay "Why Bother to Save Halloween?" Richard Seltzer writes, "Halloween is a time that reconfirms the social bond of a neighborhood (particularly the bond between different generations) by a ritual act of trade." Children confront their fear of strangers and adults have the opportunity to reconnect with their own childhoods. Perhaps all festivals of the seasons should be understood as chances to reconnect with those in our immediate world.

OCTOBER 28

Spooky sights abound at this time of year. Has anything scared you enough to give you goosebumps? The goosebumps reflex is the genetic vestige of an age-old trait; the skin lifts up hair follicles in order to gather more air around our bodies for warmth in times of stress. We see this same phenomenon at work in a dog whose hackles rise in times of danger, or a cat who's puffing himself up in order to look bigger.

In other words, goosebumps, rising hackles, and shivers down the spine may seem like signs of fear, but they're really signs that we have adapted well to cope with stress. We are stronger than we realize, and our goosebumps are the living proof.

OCTOBER 29

Carving jack o'lanterns has become a beloved Halloween ritual, but this tradition actually comes from a cautionary tale about a judgmental Creator. Irish legends tell of a man named Jack who was rejected by both God and the Devil, ultimately left to wander the earth with nothing but a coal filched from Hell, which he kept in a hollowed turnip. Allegedly the turnips were dropped from the story as the Irish immigrated to America and found the pumpkins here easier to carve.

Keep this legend in mind as you carve jack o'lanterns and remember the homeless, the disenfranchised, and the outcasts who have found no resting place in their own religion. It's fitting that we also welcome strangers to our door on Halloween night. Perhaps this is our chance to be more giving and forgiving than the deity who exiled Jack of the Lantern.

OCTOBER 30

"This Sea that bares her bosom to the moon, The winds that will be howling at all hours, And are up-gathered now like sleeping flowers, For this, for everything, we are out of tune." So writes William Wordsworth in his sonnet, "The World Is Too Much With Us." But Wordsworth gives the lie to his own despair.

The poetry with which he immortalizes the sea, the winds, and the moon demonstrates that he is far from out of tune with the earth. It may be fashionably despairing to lament how disconnected we are from nature; Wordsworth does it himself later in the poem, wishing he had some other tradition to help him glimpse Earth's power: "Great God! I'd rather be a pagan suckled in a creed outworn. . . " Yet Wordsworth proves himself a pagan in the literal sense of the word—one who finds religion in nature. This Halloween go pagan; rejoice in the moon and winds, in the rich pageant of the wilderness. Such a world cannot ever be too much with us.

OCTOBER 31

Happy New Year! Many pagans celebrate today as the dawning of the New Year—the beginning of the winter-half of the calendar, the climax of the dying summer. It is the day of the Crone, the dawning of darkness.

Called *Samhain* (pronounced "Saw-in"), this pagan holiday for venerating the dead was co-opted by the Christian culture. Hallowing the dead, the church fathers named this Hallows-Eve, which eventually morphed into Halloween. Yet the Church hasn't managed to wholly wrest this holiday from its pagan roots.

Place lights in the windows to summon your ancestors home. Set a feast out, leaving an extra helping for ghostly visitors. Tell tales of the past, and look into the future. Hallow this evening.

November

NOVEMBER 1

The natural cycle of our ancestors offered an intrinsic reason for the focus on the dead at this time of the year—it was vital in this season to thin the herds. A large burden of livestock would be impossible to support during the months of severity ahead. And the livestock themselves would provide sustenance through the winter cold. So the slaughter had to begin at this time, and people were filled with the consciousness that all things must end.

That moment of transition between death and life was so commonly seen in this season that it was impossible not to dwell on the boundary separating us from whatever comes afterward. Many people still believe that the veil can be pierced at this time. Whether or not it's true, the wheel of the seasons calls us at this time to consider with respect the mystery of what lies beyond.

NOVEMBER 2

When Mexican villagers celebrate *Los Dios de los Muertos* (the Days of the Dead), the celebrants customarily scatter finely decorated skulls made of sugar amid the feast.

Kids, of course, will eat anything. But it's striking to consider that adults, too, partake of these cranial confections. The sugar skull symbolically reminds us that it is death that gives life its sweetness. As much as we may long for immortality, without death our lives would lack flavor. Too much sugar makes sugar itself meaningless, but the sweet moments that we can snatch away from death are precious because they are limited.

NOVEMBER 3

Now that your house may be filled with Halloween candy, it's time for perspective. As much as your children's obsession (or your own) with chocolate may seem out of control, it's nothing compared to the Mayans' love of the stuff. This ancient civilization made an idol out of the cocoa bean, viewing it as a gift from the gods. Cocoa was used carefully and sparingly in mystical ceremonies, out of respect for its patron god, Ykchaua. In the later Aztec civilization, Quetzalcoatl, the god of agriculture, brought cocoa beans to his people for the same reasons that Prometheus brought fire to the Greeks—to bring them knowledge and enlightenment.

Consider what food or drink you consider a gift. What sustenance strengthens you, honors you, grounds you? Can you find nourishment that strengthens your body while it pleases your senses? You have the chance to build rituals that will help you soar rather than weigh you down.

NOVEMBER 4

At the end of October and into the beginning of November, Hindus traditionally celebrate Divali, the festival of lights. Held in honor of Lakshmi, the goddess of light, wealth, and beauty, Divali is a time of joy and festivity, commemorating the triumph of good over evil and justice over injustice. Deepa, or little lamps, are set all over the house and the streets, giving this occasion its alternate name of deepawali.

A home is transformed when it is lit by flame rather than electricity. The light shines from different angles, revealing new shapes and illuminating corners you have never really seen before, and people's faces take on a new beauty or angularity. One of the themes of Divali is the acceptance of light, and this also means accepting the new truths that unusual light brings to us.

NOVEMBER 5

Centuries ago, Mediterranean people practiced an autumnal rite called the Eleusinian Mysteries. Little is known about the specific nature of this rite, but it appears to have involved a temporary burial, recreating Persephone's journey beneath the earth to be reunited with her bridegroom Hades. Novitiates were somehow sent underground, to emerge transformed.

We don't have much taste for such practices today, but the depths of the earth still hold revelations—artifacts of our past, diamonds and other precious gems wait for us, and mysterious caves. The deeper we explore, whether in the earth or in our own hearts, the more sharply we will perceive things on the surface when we return.

NOVEMBER 6

George MacDonald's fairy tale *The Light Princess* calls our attention to a facet of nature we rarely contemplate, gravity. His heroine is born weightless and can be blown out of the window by a light breeze, sending a flock of courtiers chasing after her with nets. As she grows, she learns that her condition extends to her personality as well. When a young man comes courting, she lacks the gravity to take him seriously.

We're used to bemoaning gravity's effect on our step and our facial features as we grow older. But a fable like this teaches us that our lives would be poorer without it. In many ways, striving against the laws of nature gives our lives their meaning.

NOVEMBER 7

Two hundred years ago, London was the only city in the world that held a million people. Today there are hundreds of cities that claim at least that many residents. The majority of the world's populations lives in cities. So what does that mean for nature? Will urbanites argue for something they never experience?

It depends, of course, on how one defines *nature*. If you live in a city, you are still affected by the tides that reach your shores, the winds that carry seedlings past you, and the flowers that bloom in the least likely places, climbing up tenaciously through tarmac to reach the same sun that nourishes you.

Architecture is sometimes showy, and calls attention to itself like a class clown. Look past it at the world that really surrounds you.

NOVEMBER 8

Not that long ago kids ran loose like rabbits after school. With no parental supervision they'd bike for miles, forage in the forests, swim in the creeks.

Many parents in the United States today can't imagine letting their kids play unsupervised like this. While the reasons are sadly clear, children can't help but lose something, a sense of adventure and independence and daring, if they are always watched. Parents often feel compelled to protect their children from the same risks that they faced when they were young. Though nobody should be foolish about it, we owe it to our children to let them run manageable risks in nature now and then. Keep an eye out for the woods that will be right for your children.

NOVEMBER 9

While the Book of Genesis is very clear on the tragic outcome of Eve and Adam's adventure with the apple in the Garden of Eden, Genesis says nothing about how the fruit actually tasted. Does forbidden fruit actually taste better? If doctors urged us to eat chocolate, would we like it so much? If tomatoes were taboo, would we just have to taste them?

Today, of course, it's hard to find a good-tasting domestic tomato. Some agricultural methods don't prize flavor, but a good hothouse tomato still has a striking taste. Maybe good flavor, whether it results from taboos, or from vine-ripening, is the product of our feelings and care about the food in the first place. If we wish to savor life, we must put into it the same intensity and care.

NOVEMBER 10

An old philosophical riddle asks, "If a tree falls in the forest and nobody hears it, does it still make a sound?"

Comedian Steven Wright tells his own version: "I went out in the forest, and a tree fell; I didn't hear it."

What trees are falling that you don't hear? What will it take for you to hear them?

And once you do hear them, what will you do to prove that trees are falling when nobody else hears them?

NOVEMBER 11

As you fight off colds in the autumnal chill, remember that nature provides certain restoratives. Homeopaths have documented many exotic curatives, but even modest plants offer a certain relief. "Feeling rather sick,"

Beatrix Potter writes of Peter Rabbit, "he went to look for some parsley."

Parsley doesn't get any respect. It's used more for decoration than food, and on the few occasions when people do eat it, they fail to appreciate it. "Parsley is gharsely," writes Ogden Nash. Yet for all that we denigrate it today, the ancient Romans used parsley as a garland for heroes.

Look for the value in even the simplest substance—and maybe the search itself will be your cure.

NOVEMBER 12

As the harvest continues, its riches are more diverse than we know. Visionary companies are starting to make clothing from corn, sugar beets, and rice. Such garments would be similar in weight and behavior to polyester, but unlike synthetics, which rely on petroleum, crop-based clothing would also be biodegradable.

When we creatively tap the resources of this planet, we can also help to protect it. We may live to see a day when the wind and the sun provide us all the power we need. Walk outside and invite the wealth of the wilderness into your life—it may change things for us all.

NOVEMBER 13

As the autumn air grows chill, take this opportunity to become more mindful of the air itself. As David Abram writes in *The Spell of the Sensuous*, "the air is the most pervasive presence I can name, enveloping, embracing, and caressing me both inside and out."

We swim in the air even more deeply than we swim in water; it bathes us as it slips into our lungs and fills our hearts. It refreshes us, calms us, even startles us at times. As you bundle up against the oncoming chill, roll your sleeves up every now and then so that you can feel the prickles of the cold air against your skin, reminders of the invisible realm that gives us life.

NOVEMBER 14

Those archetypal figures of November, the pilgrims, landed near Cape Cod quite by accident; they had been headed for Virginia but made the best of their wrong turn. Centuries later, writer Henry Beston undertook his own pilgrimage to Cape Cod, chronicled in *The Outermost House*. Living on the easternmost promontory of our country for a year, he is inspired deeply by winds and poetry and silence. As he later observes, "It is only when we are aware of the earth as poetry that we truly live."

We can all be pilgrims. Like Beston at Cape Cod, like Annie Dillard at Tinker Creek, you owe yourself the opportunity to voyage into nature and reflect on what you find there. The discoveries yielded in your pilgrimages may make for a truer Thanksgiving than you have ever known.

NOVEMBER 15

Specialty stores may be starting to sell frankincense now in anticipation of the coming Christmas season, but you probably won't find stacte, onycha, and galbanum. In Exodus, God explains to Moses that these spices form a unique mixture of incense not to be used for any purpose but worship.

There are different theories about what makes incense holy. Some theorize that the smoke represents prayers spiraling up to heaven. Others feel God simply has a favorite perfume that's not to be wasted. But the most logical answer may be in the immediate experience of incense. Its aroma creates a transcendent paradox, rooting you in the present through your senses but conjuring larger worlds as its scent works upon the primitive parts of your brain. As we enter this season of incense, stay ready for transcendence.

NOVEMBER 16

The fall is a great time for bonfires, when the air is crisp and a couple of rains have reduced the risk of undergrowth catching and spreading the blaze. Bonfires work an alchemical magic as near-strangers bond around the blaze, sometimes until the wee hours of the night, happy to toast marshmallows and tell ghost stories.

Perhaps it is some Jungian memory that makes it so pleasant to gather around a fire in the dark, to relish the comfort that arises from seeing your fellows on the other side of the blaze, their faces transformed by heat and wisps of smoke. The later it gets, the harder it is not to feel that the supernatural is indeed at work in such a setting, somehow changing everyone present—sending their spirits aloft along with the embers.

NOVEMBER 17

A company called Intermountain Therapy Animals has been working with various species of dogs to help Utah children with their reading. Kids who have problems reading in classrooms are soothed when they can read to the canines, who will never correct them or tease them for their problems. Additionally, the natural effect that dogs have on the majority of people—lowering their pulse and blood rate—makes the challenge of reading less stressful.

Consider how many tasks would be easier if you allowed nature to be your companion in the work.

NOVEMBER 18

Written by early feminist and Unitarian author Lydia Marie Child, "Over the River and Through the Woods" is a beloved Thanksgiving carol—maybe the only beloved Thanksgiving carol. As with any piece from the folk tradition, it's hard to find consistent lyrics to this song; references change between Thanksgiving and Christmas, from Grandmother's house to Grandfather's house.

But the consistent thread, of course, is the title. The hearth means more when we arrive at it after journeying through the country. Even if your relatives don't live in rural splendor, the more you are alive to the power of your pilgrimage, the more you will have to give thanks for.

NOVEMBER 19

As Thanksgiving approaches, harvest imagery is every-where. Tables are decorated with cornucopia and Indian corn is hung on front doors. Yet most of us aren't exactly out there on John Deere equipment bringing in the sheaves at last.

Still, that needn't keep you from celebrating the harvest. It's a time to take stock, to appraise the progress of plans begun long ago. Use this season to reap the benefits of your actions. Hold ingatherings to connect with those you have too long neglected, or to encourage the growth of new relationships.

As Gwendolyn Brooks writes, "We are each other's harvest."

NOVEMBER 20

The full moon at this time of November is called the Beaver Moon. It may seem curious to associate the beaver, as earthy and gritty as he is, with the ethereal sights in the heavens.

But the beaver serves as a totem for the requirements of the season, managing it all with teeth, tail, and will. And so it is time to redouble your own industry, to prepare against the onslaught of winter. Is your home well-fortified? Should you be out foraging, gathering, and even dragging home the resources with which you will weather the coming cold? What must you do to keep yourself warm both physically and spiritually?

NOVEMBER 21

Pick a landscape—maybe the mountains, the beach, or the plains; it really doesn't matter as long as it's someplace that you love. Spend a day there with a camera taking photographs at regular intervals as the sun traces its way across the sky. Then look at them another day, after you've left.

You'll be astonished at the changes your pictures reveal. With each photograph, the landscape alters; there are hollows where there were none before, crags and promontories that weren't so apparent at other times. Things of beauty emerge, then disappear again.

The same is true of yourself and everyone you know. Depending on time and light, we are all capable of striking transformations.

NOVEMBER 22

Thanksgiving is a time of homecomings. Siblings, children, aunts, and uncles travel long miles to reach the site of the feast. The homestead, dull in memory, suddenly appears rich and luminous to the travelers when they arrive, even as the most prosaic household details glow with familiar memories. As you travel this Thanksgiving, enjoy the journey—but don't rush the homecoming. One of the greatest benefits of engaging in the world is the perspective it brings us when we return and see our home with new eyes. When we push ourselves onward, we learn what T. S. Eliot finally discovers: "And the end of our exploring will be to arrive where we started and know the place for the first time."

NOVEMBER 23

In Carl Phillips' poem "White Dog," he writes about releasing a white dog to run in the first snow of the year. As he lets the dog go, he can feel his affinity with his pet sundered, seeing her abruptly as just "a white dog, less white suddenly, against the snow, who won't come back. . . . and, knowing it, I release her. It's as if I release her *because* I know." Although there are some creatures and aspects of nature that we long to hold onto, but deep down we know that freedom is what they crave, what they need to survive.

Perhaps there are even aspects of your own heart that feel the same way.

NOVEMBER 24

The first story about humankind in the Bible is about people eating something they're not supposed to. In this season of bounty, as you sit down to feast, your own relationship with food may pose a similar struggle. Are you conscious of what you're eating?

The Eden story, in which we claimed free will as we gave up the garden, places our relationship with food at the heart of the matter. Why, with so many other possible laws to create, did God put a form of nourishment off limits? Perhaps it's because what we take into ourselves does create us anew. Our food's vitamins, minerals, and nutrients literally compose us. We create ourselves anew with each dinner. Bon appetit.

NOVEMBER 25

When families entertain other families at this time of year, they often wring their hands over what to do about the children. Elaborate schemes and activities are concocted to keep a squad of preschoolers occupied. But there's a simpler answer outside.

Look at that huge pile of raked leaves sitting in the yard. Diving into the pile, spilling leaves upon each other, chasing each other around the yard, raking up the pile again when it gets too scattered—theme parks have nothing on this action.

Some things are a lot simpler than we want to make them. Nature provides.

NOVEMBER 26

Musing on autumn, W. S. Merwin writes, "It is the season of migrants."

If you look overhead you may see them—the birds, the butterflies, all the creatures who choose the fall to find a safer and warmer home.

The search for the best home perplexes many of us. You may be living someplace out of necessity or habit, but do its weather and ways truly serve you? Should you consider a migration of your own? The cranes and the swallows have an internal voice that tells them when it's time to move on. Have you listened to your own inner voice lately?

NOVEMBER 27

In this era of harvest feasts it's easy to eat automatically. Food seems so abundant, we're offered and accepting meals and snacks before we know it, and suddenly we wonder how we got so stuffed.

No matter how some of us may try to separate ourselves from nature, three times a day we are reminded by our bodies that we're not so separate after all. We must regularly take into ourselves grains, fruits, meats—portions of the larger world. Think about the reasons why you eat—to replenish yourself, to strengthen your body, or to celebrate. Then add one more to the list—to reconnect.

NOVEMBER 28

When many college students return to their families for Thanksgiving they are shocked by the changed landscape. The trees are grey, barren, stark. In our memories of cherished places, we tend to picture them at their best, rich with the colors and smells of other seasons. But those elms and maples, so naked against the November sky, don't apologize. Bereft of their colors, their spines stand straight, uncompromising, even proud.

As you enter winters in your own life, there is no need to hide. You may have left behind some of the color of your youth, but take pride in your strength, your patience, and your ability to endure.

NOVEMBER 29

The rivers are starting to freeze. First little bits of glaze appear in the water, like shards of transparent glass. Day by day, the chill spreads; the glaze becomes thicker and more opaque, eventually strong enough to support a person's weight. Yet people still walk carefully on this ice, aware that underneath the water waits, biting and deep.

So it is with our hearts, hardening slowly against the bitter chill of cruelty or indifference. Perhaps no one notices at first; it can happen so slowly and we pretend everything is the same. But if you take too long to thaw, you become opaque, impenetrable. Underneath the surface, unseen currents continue to flow. Never let anyone mistake a frozen surface for the whole of you.

NOVEMBER 30

In his visionary novel, *20,000 Leagues Under the Sea*, Jules Verne created the unforgettable figure of Captain Nemo. None of the story's other characters can tell what country Nemo comes from, although in a later novel we learn he was born in India. The main reason his heritage remains obscure is that he has forsworn it. Nemo no longer recognizes the boundaries of nations and empires; he has returned to the sea to make his home.

Even as we long for world community, the lines on the map mark those nationalities, histories, and traditions that separate us. But the ocean is an empire that unites us all. Perhaps the more time we spend in this magical realm, the better the chance that the waters connecting us will grow smooth and calm.

December

DECEMBER 1

This time of year inspires the historian within each of us. Settling in for the long winter, we take a last look back.

What is the history of the land around you? You may well know some of the legal or political saga of your city—but what is the epic of the earth in your parts? How did that mountain get its name, and how many times have you climbed it? From where does that river carry its current, and where is it heading? What are the songs or stories told about this neck of the woods?

If you cannot discover the lore of your piece of the land, maybe it's time to write some of your own. You are part of the local story—you and the trees in your backyard, the sunsets outside your apartment window, the shadow you trace against the sky. This is the grist of history. Begin your ballad.

DECEMBER 2

They're getting ready to guffaw in Yamaguchi Prefecture, Japan. For over eight centuries, on the first Sunday in December, a local Shinto priest has gathered followers and set out a ritual altar bearing rice, vegetables, and other offerings. Once the meal has been consumed, he leads the collective in offering their laughter to the gods.

The origins of this practice are believed to lie in the need for a good diversion after a hard season of harvesting.

Your own life is filled with enough occasions for laughter that a special reminder is not needed. But the sound of even premeditated laughter will do you good. Nature is filled with sly jokes, and doctors have recognized the power of laughter as a restorative force; the more you appreciate nature's humor, the better off you will be.

So listen—one day a penguin walks into a bar . . . .

DECEMBER 3

Barbara Kingsolver, in her collection of essays entitled *Small Wonder*, describes the pleasures of harvesting her own food: "I've tasted heirloom vegetables with poetic names—Mortgage Lifter tomato, Moon and Stars watermelon—whose flavors most never will know because they turn to pulp and vinegar in a boxcar."

Few of us have the luxuries of time and space needed for such painstaking work. Yet whether you make your own paper, sew your own clothes, or chop your own firewood, you can find a way to nourish your own life while reconnecting with the earth. No cider tastes better than that you have squeezed yourself—literally or metaphorically.

DECEMBER 4

In his poem "Prelude to Winter," William Carlos Williams observes a motionless moth hanging in the eaves and declares that "love is a curious soft-winged thing."

Look around you in these pre-winter days, at the world bundling up—the animals whose fur grows thicker, the delicate creatures who arrange their homes just so.

Biology explains that trees are programmed to shed their leaves in order to survive the frost. But what drives biology—who does the programming? What pushes all creatures to survive and connect and scheme for next spring?

Maybe the poet is right. Maybe it is simply love.

DECEMBER 5

"I'll bring a song of love," writes Carolyn McDade, "and a rose in the wintertime."

Roses in winter are especially mysterious, their color flame-like against the wintry day. Writer Laura Shamas recommends meditating before an opening rose for fifteen minutes a day as a winter meditation. "Seeing a rose open up slowly encourages openings in our own lives," she explains. "A rose reminds us of the spring that is to come, the eternal regeneration that's part of Aphrodite's domain."

You may consider, in fact, that you yourself are the rose you contemplate. To quote another hymn: Know this rose will open.

DECEMBER 6

This day was honored centuries ago as the feast of Saint Nicholas, the progenitor of Santa Claus. Whatever your stance toward mythic Christmas figures, Nicholas also deserves notice as the patron saint of weavers, bakers, and sailors—all people who work with nature intimately, shaping it to their own ends.

Weavers take the raw fibers of the wild and shape them into recognizable patterns, seeing to one of our most basic needs. Bakers combine grains and other harvest goods with spices and herbs, firing the mixtures until they provide sustenance and flavor our lives. And sailors roam the horizons, testing the limits of our lives and bringing back their own harvests from the deep.

Even if Saint Nicholas doesn't bring presents anymore, he brings us plenty by reminding us to appreciate those craftspeople who help us make the most of this world.

DECEMBER 7

Polar bears aren't really white; they only look that way because the follicles in their fur are hollow, filled with tiny air bubbles that reflect their icy surroundings. This layer of air, carried around in their fur, insulates them against the cold and often makes them invisible to infrared photography. It's a natural defense that enables the bears to survive and thrive in the harshest of environs.

Within your native environment, perhaps you evolved some sort of adaptive tactic to help you survive in extreme weather. What is the quality within you that warms the air around you? Knowing your strengths may enable you to weather the winter—physically or emotionally—all the better.

DECEMBER 8

He was born of the ocean and the earth; his father was Poseidon and his mother was Gaia. He was unrivaled in strength as long as he maintained contact with the earth, his mother. But when a challenger had the wit to lift him off the ground and crush his ribs in midair, he finally met his death.

He was Antaeus, a little-remembered figure from the story of Hercules. How distanced are you from the planet, and how does that distance weaken you? Like Antaeus, you were born at the intersection of water and earth, and you draw your strength from the land.

If you feel you're at less than your prime, what can you do to reconnect with your roots?

DECEMBER 9

Soon it will be time to drive out the old year. Whether you do it at the winter solstice, New Year's Day, Epiphany, or Chinese New Year, you may want to start making your plans now.

Shall the old year be burned away in a ritual bonfire? Or sizzled away with fireworks? Do you want to drive it away with honking horns and clanging bells? Or write it a little farewell note and let the note blow away in the breeze?

Our packrat civilization loves to hold onto the past. Don't worry—it will always be available to you if you need it. But the future is waiting for you to claim it, and it's jealous. It doesn't like to see you still in the arms of the past. Free yourself for tomorrow.

DECEMBER 10

Once upon a time, a two-year-old girl said she saw stars in her bedroom. Her mother went and looked and saw nothing. Was her little girl feverish? Having eye problems? Her father joined them and looked where she pointed. Nothing but empty air.

Or was it empty? When the parents focused closely, they saw dust motes – brilliant white pinpoints, drifting in the beam of sunshine from their daughter's window. To her young understanding, these were stars!

Children often see such natural phenomena more easily than many of us. We adults tend to use nature as a sounding board, a place to meditate on our lives. But focus more closely and pay heed to the celestial right before your eyes.

DECEMBER 11

"Jingle Bells," the beloved winter carol, was written by Unitarian preacher James Pierpoint, ministering to a congregation in sunny Savannah, Georgia, at the time. Perhaps his recollections of winter sleigh rides were all the stronger because of their absence, strong enough to inspire one of the most enduring holiday songs.

What rides and walks through the wild are calling to you from the recesses of your memory? We all have treasured memories of some encounter with the wilderness, an encounter that seems distant and maybe even beyond recapturing. It doesn't have to be romantic or pristine; "Jingle Bells" describes a couple tumbling into a snowbank when their horse loses his footing. Maybe the accident is what makes the whole trip so sweet. What song is your own heart singing about your days or nights adventuring through the woods?

DECEMBER 12

Winter is a time of clouds, some bearing hail, sleet, or snow, while others are simply the ceiling of an overcast day. Denise Levertov's poem "Clouds" describes them "in pomp advancing, pursuing the fallen sun." The ongoing procession of cumulus, stratus, cirrus, and nimbus feels in this season like a ceaseless pageant. Rather than playing the Rorschach game and asking what a cloud looks like, maybe we should be wondering where it is going.

The parade of clouds moves on, sometimes lazily, sometimes with apparent urgency. And as it does, it gives us a gift, the illusion that maybe we're not part of the parade ourselves. We can lie back and watch the clouds and imagine for a moment that we're mere spectators who can step in and out of the procession at will. But of course, like the clouds, our spirits are blown onward whether we acknowledge it or not. Have you asked yourself lately where you're going?

DECEMBER 13

The shortening of the daily cycle gives rise to festivals of light around the world. Today is Saint Lucia's Day, a traditional Swedish festival that combines pagan heritage with Christian legend. Lucia herself had little to do with light and winter; she was a Christian martyr beheaded in the days when Christians faced horrific persecutions. But because her name is Latin for light, the Vikings who converted to Christianity infused their solstice service with the personage of this beloved saint.

The Scandinavian image of a young woman in a white robe and a wreath of burning candles is a compelling image. It is a day to let everyone's light shine— and perhaps to wonder how we can bring light and sustenance into each other's lives more often.

DECEMBER 14

The next time you brew yourself a hot drink to ward off the chill of a winter night, take a good look at the dregs you leave at the bottom of your mug. According to some traditions, they can tell your future.

Schemes for reading tea leaves or coffee grounds vary. Some tasseographers, as they are called, interpret the lines and swirls according to where they fall in the bottom of the cup. Others assign meaning to pictures that they discern like Rorschach blots in the leaves or the grounds.

Whether you subscribe to the idea of fortune-telling or not, perhaps your future becomes clearest when you look at what you leave behind.

DECEMBER 15

When it's cold and wet outside, our natural instinct is to sequester ourselves in our homes, protected against the elements. As cozy as this may be, it can be lonely too. Maybe the turtle has something to say to you.

Turtles take their homes with them wherever they go. This must be a useful strategy, because they're among the longest-lived creatures on earth. Quiet and unassuming, turtles still possess a sharp bite and can survive even when seriously wounded. Their carapaces give them both the protection and the strength to go where other animals their size could never dare.

Rather than getting out of your shell, maybe you should get your shell out and about more often.

DECEMBER 16

Time is on our minds as December wends toward its finish. Often it seems impossible that the year could be so close to its end. Where did the time go and how could we have failed to notice? The minutes and the hours seem like stern taskmasters, bearing down on us so inexorably and then leaving before we're ready.

The ancient Japanese had a more gentle way of telling time. Building on Chinese skill with incense, they developed clocks that told time according to the number of incense sticks that were burned. This method was so accurate that geishas could be paid by the amount of incense that was burned during a client's visit.

What if you made an appointment not for four o'clock . . . but for when the sandalwood was finished burning? What if you started dinner not at six-thirty . . . but with the jasmine? Time might offer you a reunion with the sensual world.

DECEMBER 17

Winter is the best time to harvest willow, the revered wood of the druids. The sap is at rest, and so the bark will stay intact as the wood dries. The brush growing around the trees won't get in your way, allowing the willow to offer itself up with both its full strength and its full flexibility.

Winter's frost now may be wearing at your own vigor and diminishing your limberness. The lesson of the willow is not just about physical flexibility but about willingness to change: when your beliefs become hardened and brittle, they're likely to snap under stress.

DECEMBER 18

Isaac Asimov's classic science fiction story "Nightfall" tells of a world on which daylight lasts for centuries. When the cycle finally comes to an end, and night is coming for the first time in living memory, people start to panic.

Maybe we're lucky to have a special balance of day and night. We can't be spoiled by the long days of summer, for we know they won't last long, nor are we dismayed by the long nights of winter, for we know they're just a phase.

All life, in fact, is a phase. A new one begins for you tomorrow. Embrace it.

DECEMBER 19

Tomorrow begins the winter solstice. In the Northern Hemisphere, there is less sunlight on the solstice than on any other day of the year. "The days are getting shorter," schoolchildren are told, but on the stern black clocks in their classrooms, the second hand seems to tick away at its usual laborious pace. It's a while before kids learn that some folks consider a day to be twenty-four hours (with an additional second added now and then to keep up with nature), while others mean a day only to be that period of time when the sun is out.

The loss of the sun was a true bane to our distant ancestors, who relied on its heat and safety. We, however, need not be daunted by the growing night. We can trade the old traditional, "In the Bleak Midwinter," for a hymn like "Dark of Winter" by Shelley Jackson Denham: "Gentle darkness, soft and still, bring your quiet to me." The growing darkness can be a blessing. It can let you focus in ways the hectic days do not allow. You can find serenity in its silence.

DECEMBER 20

Today marks the actual beginning of the Winter Solstice, when the sun is most remote from us. Ancient festivals used this day to call back the sun, whether in the form of the Persian god Mithras or the Scandinavian Saint Lucia. You too can call back the sun. Walk outside and take a look at the skies. Thank them for the canopy they provide. Blow a kiss to the sun, even if it's hidden behind clouds, for that kiss will be returned as the sun brings its radiance back to full majesty.

Remember the George Harrison song "Here Comes the Sun"—the simplest of melodies, the plainest of lyrics. But to recognize this basic truth, to honor our reliance on the sun, what more words are needed?

"Here comes the sun, and I say, it's all right."

DECEMBER 21

The Winter Solstice climaxes today, a day known in many cultures as *Yule*. Nobody's sure of the exact etymology of the word *Yule*, but many have speculated that it's related to the word *wheel*. The cycle of the seasons is a wheel, and at Yule we take special notice of how the wheel turns again.

With a new year dawning, reflect on the words of Robert D. Richardson Jr. in his biography of Ralph Waldo Emerson: "Any book may be read, any idea thought, any action taken. Anything that has ever been possible to human beings is possible to most of us every time the clock strikes six in the morning. On a day no different from the one now breaking, Shakespeare sat down to begin Hamlet . . . ."

As you begin again today, remember that you may begin again every day.

DECEMBER 22

In Iceland, the Yule Cat skulks around and gobbles up those who have neglected their chores. This harshness is the rare exception among Yule celebrations, however, for Yule is a time for singing songs, decorating homes, and burning the traditional Yule log to symbolize the end of the old year and the birth of the new.

This event is well known to us from the most pagan of holiday carols, "Deck the Halls," which not only tells us to hang holly throughout our homes, join with others in song and old stories, dress up in party clothes, and have a good laugh, but also to "see the blazing Yule before us." What would it mean if you regularly set fire to the past? What if you left all your old joys and regrets in the ashes and met the future on its own terms? The opportunity is now.

DECEMBER 23

At Solstice, at Yuletide, and at Christmas, families regularly bring the wilderness into their homes by setting pine boughs on their mantles, hanging wreaths, symbols of the nature cycles that nourish us, on their doors; and even erecting trees in a place of pride within their homes. The trees are festooned with all manner of ornaments, from popcorn and berries to glowing orbs and figurines to strings of lights.

The evergreens—the pines and firs that provide winter color when the rest of the landscape is white and gray during this harsh time of year—remind us that life perseveres. Even in the most trying of times, the trees grow. And so do you.

DECEMBER 24

In many lands, today is celebrated as Christmas Eve. No matter how you regard the divinity of the great teacher Jesus, the account of his birth is striking. Picture the baby being born in the manger—amid the smells and the deep breaths of the livestock. Imagine the shepherds searching the night sky for hope. Envision the wise men bringing precious metals and incense to the infant's side.

Do you celebrate Christmas Eve in the immediacy of Creation or in the cozy confines to which you are accustomed? Consider what might happen if you took a break from your usual revelry and instead reveled in the sounds and the smells of the world outside your window. Consider lighting incense—gathering wisdom— and studying the stars. Perhaps the gifts of nature that surrounded the baby Jesus taught him to love so greatly.

DECEMBER 25

Today is the day chosen to represent the birth of Jesus, but for the first two centuries after his death, nobody knew when Jesus actually entered the world. Priests of that time actually discouraged people from investigating when Jesus was born, preferring to downplay his lowly origins. Nevertheless, we might recall that many special children definitely were born this day. Clara Barton, founder of the American Red Cross, celebrated her birthday on December 25, as did physicist Isaac Newton.

Whether or not it's true that Newton "discovered" gravity when an apple fell on his head, the tale holds an enduring fascination. Genesis uses the apple to symbolize man's fall, but Newton rehabilitates the apple as an opportunity to understand the world around us. Have an apple today, and remember that our understanding of nature may be changed by any child born today or tomorrow.

In the words of Sophia Lyon Fahs, "Each night a child is born is a holy night."

DECEMBER 26

In 1966, Dr. Maulana Karenga created the holiday Kwanzaa, drawing upon ancient traditions from Egypt to Yorubaland. But because the word *Kwanzaa* is a Swahili term meaning "first fruits," this celebration (like so many in December) is also connected to the earth.

Kwanzaa is a time of reverence and gratitude for the beauty and bounty of creation.

Whatever your cultural or ethnic background, join today in appreciation of what creation has brought to all of us.

DECEMBER 27

David Oates' *Paradise Wild: Reimagining American Nature* offers a new way to get back to nature. Haunted by the Eden myth as we are, Oates argues, we keep working to transport ourselves to the wilderness, and yet we often find ourselves oddly unsatisfied upon our arrival. Oates' prescription is to realize that "we are already inside of nature, we ourselves are the inside, the inwardness of nature, if anyone is."

The more you care for yourself and your world, the more you roll up your sleeves to practice regeneration and rebirth, the more you recreate Eden in your very self. The results will emanate outward in ways you cannot imagine. During this season, when a garden seems so very distant, find your inner garden.

DECEMBER 28

Winter is a time of regeneration. To consider regeneration literally, we must look to nature. Starfish can grow back a lost arm, as can spiders. Lizards who lose their tails in battle can sometimes regrow them. And shark grow new teeth when they lose old ones, sometimes growing up to 24,000 teeth in their lifetime.

While we lack the obvious advantages these animals

enjoy, our bodies also have a remarkable capacity for healing. Automatically, every night as we sleep, our cells repair damage from the previous day. And as we look forward to a new year, the late December is an ideal time to rest and recuperate, either from physical efforts or from the stresses of life. We may not have caves to help us hibernate and recharge ourselves for the future, but we do have our homes and hearths.

DECEMBER 29

Birth is celebrated at Yuletide, whether it be the birth of the new season, the Sun King, the Christ-child, or the coming year. When was the last time you saw a baby, either human or animal? When was the last time you held one in your arms? Have you ever?

Men in our culture are not encouraged to coddle babies or delight in childhood, so it's possible for many men to grow well into adulthood and never cradle a baby against their chests. In centuries past, when extended families were the norm, such an outcome was nearly impossible. Yet today, a chance to experience the wonder of birth is still denied to so many. If you know someone with a baby, look at it closely. Offer to hold it. Drink in the amazement of a baby's vulnerability, a baby's power, a baby's potential. If you have a baby yourself, take a moment soon to let others take in the wonder. The more we appreciate birth, the more we will encourage life.

DECEMBER 30

The science fiction writer Ursula K. LeGuin has said, "Every time we light a candle, we cast a shadow." The shadows are longer at this time of year, but they are a natural consequence of light, and enable us to appreciate light all the more.

We are more in shadow now, in the northern hemisphere, because the southern half of the planet is more in light. Our winter is their summer, their time of greatest sun. And in order for us to enjoy summer, they must endure winter. The names of seasons are only manmade concepts—your season depends on where you actually sit on the planet.

Have you ever seen the maps that show the southern hemisphere at the top of the planet? The northern perspective is only that—a perspective. Just as every light is defined in part by the darkness surrounding it, let us remember that there are two sides to everything—at least!

DECEMBER 31

As many countries celebrate the end of the year today, you may see an image that hearkens back to our agrarian past. The Reaper, symbol of the closing year, is an arcane figure to many today, since very few city dwellers and suburbanites ever see someone using a scythe. Because urban life has disconnected us from the cycle of growth and harvest, the significance of the Reaper is diminished for us.

Yet reaping is vital to our lives. Look back at the food on your table and consider how it was harvested. Someone judged when the fruit and grains were most ripe and cut them down for you before decay could set in.

Consider this not as a time of endings and beginnings but rather as a time of ripeness. What if now is the moment to seize the fruit from the tree?

ACKNOWLEDGMENTS

Special thanks to those writers who blaze literary trails into the wild and whom I have quoted within these pages.

Added personal thanks to editor Mary Benard; the Rev. Anne Felton Hines, minister of Emerson Unitarian Universalist Church in Canoga Park, CA; Lisa Willner, Director of Religious Education at First Unitarian Church, Louisville, KY; Julie Brams-Prudeaux; Mehrdad Haghi; Laura Shamas; and most of all to Barbara, Madeleine, and Olivia Calvi, the three lights of my day.